MODIFIED ESSAY QUESTIONS
FOR THE MRCGP EXAMINATION

Modified Essay Questions for the MRCGP Examination

EDITED BY T.S. MURRAY
MD, PhD, FRCGP, FRCP(G),
FRCP(E), DRCOG
Professor of General Practice,
University of Glasgow
West of Scotland Regional Adviser
in General Practice

SECOND EDITION

b

Blackwell
Science

© 1986, 1995 by
Blackwell Science Ltd
Editorial Offices:
Osney Mead, Oxford OX2 0EL
25 John Street, London WC1N 2BL
23 Ainslie Place, Edinburgh EH3 6AJ
238 Main Street, Cambridge
  Massachusetts 02142, USA
54 University Street, Carlton
  Victoria 3053, Australia

Other Editorial Offices:
Arnette Blackwell SA
  1, rue de Lille, 75007 Paris
France

Blackwell Wissenschafts-Verlag GmbH
  Kurfürstendamm 57
  10707 Berlin, Germany

Feldgasse 13, A-1238 Wien
Austria

First published 1986
Reprinted 1987, 1992
Second edition 1995

Set by Semantic Graphics, Singapore
Printed and bound in Great Britain
by Hartnolls Ltd, Bodmin, Cornwall

DISTRIBUTORS

Marston Book Services Ltd
PO Box 87
Oxford OX2 0DT
(*Orders*: Tel: 01865 791155
        Fax: 01865 791927
        Telex: 837515)

North America
Blackwell Science, Inc.
238 Main Street
Cambridge, MA 02142
(*Orders*: Tel: 800 215-1000
          617 876-7000
          Fax: 617 492-5263)

Australia
Blackwell Science Pty Ltd
54 University Street
Carlton, Victoria 3053
(*Orders*: Tel: 03 9347 0300
          Fax: 03 9349 3016)

A catalogue record for this title
is available from the British Library

ISBN 0 86542 646 5

Library of Congress
Cataloging-in-Publication Data

Modified essay questions for the
MRCGP examination / edited by T.S.
Murray. — 2nd ed.
     p. cm.
   Includes bibliographical references
   and index.
   ISBN 0-86542-646-5
   1. Internal medicine—Examinations,
   questions, etc. I. Murray,
T. S. (T. Stuart)
RC58.M59 1995
616'.0076—dc20
DNLM/DLC
for Library of Congress   95-34949
                                    CIP

Contents

List of Contributors

All are current or recent examiners for the MRCGP

L. M. CAMPBELL FRCGP, *Assistant Adviser in Assessment, West of Scotland Postgraduate Education Board, Honorary Clinical Senior Lecturer, University of Glasgow, Department of Postgraduate Medical Education and General Practitioner, Kirkintilloch, Glasgow*

M. H. KELLY PhD, FRCGP, *Assistant Adviser, Department of Postgraduate Medical Education, University of Glasgow and General Practitioner, Glasgow*

A. C. K. LOCKIE BSc (Hons), FRCGP, DRCOG, MICGP, *Examiner for the MRCGP and Past Convenor MEQ, Chairman Exam Test Committee: Diploma in Family Practice RCGP (Kuwait) and General Practitioner, Stratford-upon-Avon*

T. S. MURRAY MD, PhD, FRCGP, FRCP(G), FRCP(E), DRCOG, *Professor of General Practice, University of Glasgow, West of Scotland Regional Adviser in General Practice*

J. L. OXENBURY MRCGP, DCH, DRCOG, *General Practitioner, Camberley, Surrey and General Practice Tutor, Frimley Park District*

G. D. ROBERTS MRCP, FRCGP, DCH, *General Practitioner, Camberley, Surrey and Honorary Senior Lecturer in General Practice, St George's Hospital Medical School, London*

F. M. SULLIVAN PhD, FRCP, MRCGP, *Senior Lecturer in General Practice, University of Glasgow and General Practitioner, Blantyre, Lanarkshire*

L. M. TAPPER-JONES MD, FRCGP, DRCOG, DCH, MFFP, *Senior Lecturer in General Practice, University of Wales, College of Medicine, Cardiff*

G. B. TAYLOR FRCGP, DRCOG, *General Practitioner, Guide Post Health Centre, Northumberland, Associate Regional Adviser, Postgraduate Institute, Newcastle upon Tyne*

C. R. WHITEHOUSE MA, FRCGP, DRCOG, DCH, *Professor of Teaching Medicine in the Community, University of Manchester and Principal in General Practice, Manchester*

Preface to the Second Edition

The Membership of the Royal College of General Practitioners (MRCGP) examination remains popular and the MEQ continues to be an important component of the written section. Marked changes have taken place in the MEQ since the first edition of the book and these will be described in a separate chapter. The first examination for membership of the Royal College of General Practitioners was held in November 1965, when five candidates sat the examination. Council decided in 1968 that only candidates who had passed the examination would be admitted for membership. The first compulsory examination, held in November 1968, attracted 32 candidates and by 1971 the annual total exceeded 163. Within 4 years this had risen to an annual total of 400 and within a further 4 years to over 1200. Currently over 1600 candidates each year are examined for the MRCGP.

Preparation for the exam with examples of materials used is a constant request from those sitting. The written component of the MRCGP consists of three papers, an MCQ, an MEQ and a critical reading paper. The MEQ tests problem-solving and decision-making in a broad range of clinical settings and also looks at candidates' clinical skills and attitudes, although the latter are also examined in different parts of the examination, e.g. the orals.

The MEQ deals with a number of real patients in general practice situations which present the candidate with a test that requires thought and experience. It also covers management and ethical issues. Anyone sitting the exam will benefit from working through the problems in the book, and other doctors who are involved in teaching will also benefit as the problems are related to everyday general practice.

All 10 contributors are current or recent MRCGP examiners and all continue to be involved in teaching. Each person has produced two surgeries, each involving 10 situations.

List of Abbreviations

AA	Alcoholics Anonymous
ACEI	angiotensin-converting enzyme inhibitor
AIDS	acquired immune deficiency syndrome
Anti-D	Anti-rhesus antigen D
BASICS	British Association for Immediate Care
BNF	*British National Formulary*
BP	blood pressure
BTS	British Thoracic Society
CF	cystic fibrosis
CHD	coronary heart disease
CME	continuing medical education
COAD	chronic obstructive airways disease
CPN	community psychiatric nurse
CPR	cardiopulmonary resuscitation
CRQ	critical reading question
CVA	cerebrovascular accident
CXR	chest X-ray
D and C	dilation and curettage
DM	diabetes mellitus
DSS	Department of Social Security
DU	duodenal ulcer
ECG	electrocardiogram
ESR	erythrocyte sedimentation rate
FBC	full blood-count
FHSA	Family Health Service Authority
FP1	NHS prescription
GI	gastrointestinal
H_2	histamine 2
HbA_1C	haemoglobin A_1C
HIV	human immunodeficiency virus
HRT	hormone replacement therapy
IHD	ischaemic heart disease
IQ	intelligence quotient

IUCD	intrauterine contraceptive device
IVP	intravenous pyelogram
LMC	local medical committee
LMP	last menstrual period
MCQ	multiple choice questionnaire
MDI	metered dose inhaler
MEQ	modified essay question
ME	myalgic encephalomyelitis
MI	myocardial infarction
MS	multiple sclerosis
MSU	midstream urine
MSSU	midstream sample of urine
OCP	oral contraceptive pill
OTC	over the counter
PACT	prescribing analysis and cost
PCC	postcoital contraception
PCP	postcoital protection
PEF	peak expiratory flow
PHCT	primary health care team
PMH	past medical history
STD	sexually transmitted disease
TFT	thyroid function test
UTI	urinary tract infection

1

A Description of the Work of a General Practitioner

The general practitioner is a licensed medical graduate who gives personal, primary and continuing care to individuals, families and a practice population, irrespective of age, sex and illness. It is the synthesis of these functions which is unique. They will attend their patients in the consulting room and in their home and sometimes in a clinic or a hospital. Their aim is to make early diagnoses. They will include and integrate physical, psychological and social factors in their considerations about health and illness. This will be expressed in the care of their patients. They will make an initial decision about every problem which is presented to them as doctors. They will undertake the continuing management of their patients with chronic, recurrent or terminal illness. Prolonged contact means that they can use repeated opportunities to gather information at a pace appropriate to each patient and build up a relationship of trust which they can use professionally. They will practise in co-operation with other colleagues, medical and non-medical. They will know how and when to intervene through treatment, prevention and education to promote the health of their patients and their families. They will recognize that they also have a professional responsibility to the community.

EDUCATIONAL AIMS

From this broad description of the general practitioner are derived the following educational aims which should be attained by the time a doctor enters independent practice. Many of them are shared with other doctors.

They are arranged in three groups:
- those mainly involving knowledge;
- those mainly involving skills;
- those mainly involving attitudes.

All three groups are equally important.

At the conclusion of the vocational training programme, the doctor should be able to demonstrate the following abilities.

1 Knowledge

• That they have sufficient knowledge of disease processes, particularly of common diseases, chronic diseases and those which endanger life or have serious complications or consequences.

• That they understand the opportunities, methods and limitations of prevention, early diagnosis and management in the setting of general practice.

• Their understanding of the way in which interpersonal relationships within the family can cause health problems or alter their presentation, course and management, just as illness can influence family relationships.

• An understanding of the social and environmental circumstances of their patients and how they may affect a relationship between health and illness.

• Their knowledge and appropriate use of the wide range of interventions available to them.

• That they understand the ethics of their profession and their importance for the patient.

• That they understand the basic methods of research as applied to general practice.

• An understanding of medicosocial legislation and of the impact of this on their patients.

2 Skills

• How to form diagnoses which take account of physical, psychological and social factors.

• That they understand the use of epidemiology and probability in their everyday work.

• Understanding and use of the factor 'time' as a diagnostic, therapeutic and organizational tool.

• That they can identify persons at risk and take appropriate action.

• That they can make relevant initial decisions about every problem presented to them as doctors.

• The capacity to co-operate with medical and non-medical professionals.

• Knowledge and appropriate use of the skills of practice management.

3 Attitudes

• A capacity for empathy and for forming a specific and effective relationship with patients and for developing a degree of self-understanding.

• How their recognition of the patient as a unique individual modifies the ways in which they elicit information and make hypotheses about the nature of a patient's problems and their management.

• That they understand that helping patients to solve their own problems is a fundamental therapeutic activity.

• That they recognize that they can make a professional contribution to the wider community.

• That they are willing and able critically to evaluate their own work.

• That they recognize their own need for continuing education and critical reading of medical information.

THE LEEUWENHURST STATEMENT

The following forms the basis of the Leeuwenhurst Statement 1974.

The Joint Committee for Postgraduate Training for General Practice have suggested a number of attributes.

Attributes of the doctor completing vocational training for general practice

A general practitioner is expected to provide comprehensive primary medical care for individual patients and anticipatory health care for the practice population.

The expectation of patients and professional colleagues is therefore that the future general practitioner will be:

• accessible and available to patients;

• skilled in diagnosis, management and all other aspects of the consultation;

• knowledgeable about clinical general practice;

• skilled in communication;

• appreciative of the importance of teamwork in primary health care;

• able to organize and manage a practice;

• able to understand the need to continue their professional development through activities such as: the gaining of further clinical

experience, continuing education, research and other professional
responsibilities;
• committed to the principles and practice of performance review;
• able to understand the ethical principles which govern the profession and committed to observing them;
• competent in the use of resources available to help patients;
• able to show a caring attitude to patients and families.

2

The MRCGP Examination

The College publication which is a guide for candidates and teachers (Moore and Pereira Gray, 1994) lists five reasons why general practitioners should take the MRCGP examination.

• *Personal satisfaction*. Passing the exam brings considerable personal professional pride to young doctors and they also receive the seal of approval from the Royal College that they have reached a high standard. Their satisfaction is also considered important by all those who are involved in their training process.

• *Career advancement*. All those who aspire to leading positions within the general practice branch of the profession need to have passed the examination.

• *Quality marker*. The exam is currently peer-referenced, with a constant 75% passing. Success does mean that the examinee has reached the quality standard.

• *Financial advantage*. The possession of the MRCGP may mean cheaper medical insurance with some of the professional indemnity services.

• *Supporting the discipline*. Being a member of the College is part of the collective professional responsibility of general practitioners to support their Royal College.

There are three written papers (Lockie, 1990), the MCQ paper being the principal test of factual knowledge in the exam. It now contains a variable number of stems, each with three to six items relating to it. The total number of items is approximately 360 and they are designed to cover the vast area of knowledge required for general practice. Within the MCQ paper there are now several extended matching questions whose purpose is to allow candidates to apply their knowledge to situations likely to be found in practice and to apply this probability to their decision-making. The questions consist of a series of between three and six clinical situations set out in two or three sentences each with a list of possible diagnoses. The task is to match the most likely diagnostic option to each situation or item.

5

The CRQ paper consists of five parts, each with two questions. This tests candidates' ability to read, analyse and draw conclusions from written material relevant to their work.

The MEQ paper traditionally dealt with a central patient and family who developed a series of medical problems and situations over time. The number of pages in these MEQs could vary between seven and 10 but all were related to the presenting clinical situation (Lockie, 1990). Two hours and 20 minutes are allowed for the MEQ paper. Examiners were aware that the traditional MEQ paper was not representative of the everyday situation which trainees meet, as it could present over months or years. More recently, the examinations have tended to be of a surgery situation where a clinical or management scenario is dealt with as a single item. Analysis of the previous format had indicated that candidates' performance might vary considerably from one scenario to the next and if the candidate got the first part of the traditional MEQ wrong then they were disadvantaged for the remainder of the paper. It was felt that to increase the reliability and validity the number of questions should be increased to 10 and there should be a single marker following the marking schedule. Answers that are expected should contain those ideas which a general practitioner should have at his or her immediate command in actual practice rather than a full and detailed explanation of the subject. The paper is presented in a stapled leaflet with each page containing one situation with the question at the top of the page. The pages are then separated and sent to different examiners for marking.

Once the written papers are marked, all those who are above one standard deviation below the mean mark (around 85% of candidates) are invited for orals. Overall 75% will pass the examination.

REFERENCES

Lockie C. (ed.) (1990) *Examination for MRCGP*. Occasional Paper No. 46, Royal College of General Practitioners, London.

Moore R. (1994) *The MRCGP examination*. Preface by Denis Pereira Gray. Royal College of General Practitioners, London.

3

Methods of Marking MEQs and Explanation of Constructs

The questions are marked using a schedule developed by those examiners who are marking each question. In each MEQ there are normally 10 questions, each marked by a group of five or six examiners. This has recently been increased to 12 questions. These are prepared individually by the examiners and refined and finalized at the annual workshop. There should be essential parts in a good answer and these essential features or constructs are what are now used. There are usually between three and five for each question. Within the construct there are essential points. The examiner's task is to see whether the candidate has identified the various constructs in the schedule and awards a mark for each one according to how well it has been described or discussed, with 5 being the maximum mark obtained if it is fully and rationally dealt with. The answer should be what is comprehensive and practical in a 12-minute situation. These are given in the answers and would attract the maximum score (5).

A paper on construct marking (R. Neighbour, personal communication, 1995) restates that the MEQ is to test candidates' decision-making, their ability to translate theoretical knowledge into practice, their attitudes, values and priorities, their ability to deal with complex and unexpected situations and their understanding of the doctor's role in all its context.

A construct is an independent variable, a theme, a strand or a dimension. A construct should be independent and a candidate could score highly in one construct and low in another. Examples of constructs are: consultation skills; follow-up arrangements; awareness of ethical considerations; clinical safety; caritas; sense of genuine caring or empathy. When dealing with a situation, candidates should ask themselves the following questions.

• What are the essential and critical features of this situation?
• What could a good doctor do in this case?
• What alternatives for action are there here?
• What are the reasons and justifications for the action proposed?

On the day, the following ideas may help.

• Read the instructions at the beginning of the paper carefully.

• Keep track of time as you work through the paper.

• Do not spend so much time on one question that you run short on others.

• You must answer all the questions.

• Omission of one item will lose one-tenth of your possible marks.

• Read each question carefully, word by word and clause by clause. They have been very carefully constructed and virtually every word is significant.

• Place yourself into the scene depicted in the question and consider all the characters, whether they are explicitly mentioned or not.

• Ask yourself: 'What do the examiners have in mind in this question?', 'What are its essential and critical features?', 'Where is it capable of leading my thoughts?'

• Write legibly; fewer words written slowly may say more than many in haste.

• Make your answers meaningful.

• Set the answers out clearly and tidily.

• Remember to keep your answers on the relevant page and do not refer to other pages. Pages go to different groups of examiners, who will not understand your linked statements.

• You will see in the examples following that occasionally unconventional questions are asked and this should not be a problem to candidates whose outlook and experience are broad and whose knowledge and perception extend beyond what has been addressed previously.

Remember you answer each item as completely as the time allows: the constructs are broad and they are the areas marks are given for.

At the end of each surgery there is a commentary on some of the constructs. You will see from these that the range of constructs is vast, representing the breadth of thinking which is required for problem-solving and decision-making. The problems in the book should be discussed with peers, trainers and other general practitioners. Ability to solve problems and to make decisions are two of the most important characteristics of a general practitioner.

THE QUESTIONS

The questions prepared by the 10 contributors cover vast areas of general practice and you will note that with 10 people working independently the degree of duplication and overlap is tiny. Those people preparing the questions have developed their own constructs within their own local situation. In all situations the ideal is given and this is what would obtain maximum marks. Remember that the constructs are those thought essential by the examiners and that they cover the relevant items. At the end of each surgery, there will be a commentary after the answers.

MEQ 1

1.1 Susan, aged 12, has cerebral palsy with severe dystonic tetraplegia following birth injury. She has had recurrent severe chest infections. In recent months swallowing has become so difficult and dangerous that she now has a gastrostomy tube by which means she is fed. She also has convulsions and requires anti-epileptic therapy. There are two younger children under school age in the family and the mother is separated from her husband. What are the management issues in her case?

1.2 You are invited to give a talk to a mother-and-toddler group on the subject of child health. List the issues you would raise.

1.3 Amanda, aged 3 months, normal birth weight and history, attends your clinic with her mother. The mother states that Amanda has had a constant cough, is always breathless and often has sputum. She frequently sneezes and appears to have a blocked nose. Her bowels are loose. On examination she is marasmic and has considerable respiratory distress, with many adventitious sounds in the chest. This is the first occasion you have met this child with her mother and no previous notes are available. You wish to explain matters to Amanda's mother. What points would you propose to discuss?

1.4 Mr and Mrs Williams, aged 27, live in a large town which has a general and obstetric hospital. Mrs Williamson comes home from the obstetric hospital, having had her second child, Ian, birth weight 3.5 kg, normal delivery, aged 3 days. The midwife informs you that the baby is jaundiced. What issues does this present?

1.5 A brother and sister, John and Emma, aged 4 and 6, are brought up to you by their anxious mother. She is on holiday visiting elderly grandparents. She reports that the children have spots on their hands and feet and the perianal area. The mother demands to know what is wrong. How would you progress?

11

1.6 A schoolgirl, Sharon, aged 15, is brought to see you by two of her schoolmates in your capacity as school doctor. The schoolgirl has hidden the fact that she might be pregnant from everyone except her schoolmates, and she panicked when she developed a rash which seemed very like the description of German measles which had been discussed in class by the school nurse as part of an educational programme. All three girls are with you together in the surgery. What issues arise?

1.7 Rupert, aged 12, is brought to see you by his mother, who is a lecturer in genetics. He is refusing to play rugby because he says his back is persistently sore. Rupert's mother reminds you that her daughter developed scoliosis, which was not recognized at an early stage. How would you proceed?

1.8 You live in a small town near a major paediatric hospital. Joseph, a boy of 12 years, attends you as an emergency. He has a deep knee laceration, and is reluctant to explain the origin. You know him well – he is fostered by your neighbours. You feel you could stitch the laceration but it is about the limit of your skills. The boy smells strongly of alcohol. What are the issues?

1.9 The foster-parents suddenly arrive – both are clearly intoxicated. They state that the boy stole a motor scooter. The boy shouts that this is not true and viciously attacks his foster-parents. How would you handle the situation?

1.10 Your female trainee in the third week of her traineeship tells you that she is pregnant. Discuss the issues.

MEQ 2

2.1 In your capacity as school medical officer to a primary school in a small town the headmaster asks you to see a young boy, John, just started school, aged 5, who is extremely disruptive in the classroom. He is being fostered with a view to adoption. The foster-mother has a full-time job as a social work administrator and the foster-father is based at home as a commercial artist and largely looks after the boy. The boy has been in the household for 6 months. How would you handle this situation?

2.2 William, aged 6 years, is brought to see you by his mother. He has not been going to school for several weeks because the other children have been shouting 'smelly' at him because he had soiled pants. This is the first time you have met the mother and boy. List the information which you would wish to obtain before completion of the first consultation.

2.3 You are asked to give general advice about dental hygiene for infants and preschool-age children. List the issues you would raise.

2.4 Billy, aged 14, is brought to see you by his mother. He is a footballer of considerable quality and the next day is due to go on a special training camp for exceptional young footballers – an opportunity which will probably not arise again. He proves to have undoubted shingles (herpes zoster) of the left abdominal wall. The lesions have been appearing for about 2–3 days. List the issues in management of the condition.

2.5 A 37-year-old married woman, who is a teacher married to a dentist, attends your surgery because she thinks she may have become pregnant for the first time; she has been married for 7 years. She asks about the value of chorion villus sampling and, if she is pregnant, if this technique is helpful in assessment. Discuss the various problems presented.

2.6 Ann, an only child, aged 14 years, is brought to see you by her father, who is divorced. He is a lorry-driver. For the past 6 weeks she has had a pain in her wrists, knees, shoulders and ankles. She feels nauseated and sweats at night excessively, and has not attended school. What are the issues for the consultation?

2.7 In your capacity as general practitioner you see a 6-week-old infant, one of twins, with an illness that seems to be of a simple, viral, upper respiratory tract nature, very late in the evening. What are the issues?

2.8 Six hours later you are called suddenly by the mother, who says that the infant is dead in bed. You attend immediately and confirm that this is the case. Describe the actions required.

2.9 At the end of the evening, when everybody else except the doctor has gone home and you still have four patients to see, the phone rings. It is Michael Sweeney, a 72-year-old retired miner, asking for advice about pains in his chest that have been coming and going for the past 2 to 3 days. How do you deal with this phone call?

2.10 Your trainee has been causing concern by being late for surgeries and unavailable when on call. You have discussed this with him and he denies there is a problem. What options are available in dealing with the problem?

MEQ 3

3.1 Jim Milroy is a 42-year-old rep. He has recently had a bronchoscopy which shows a bronchial carcinoma. He has arranged the consultation to discuss the outcome of the test. He attended as a day patient and is unaware of the result. However, he does admit to being worried. How would you handle this situation?

3.2 Fred Abbott is a 14-year-old who has been truanting from school. He calls without an appointment and demands to see you. He admits that he is addicted to heroin and wishes to be weaned off the drug. How would you manage the consultation?

3.3 Your next patient is Annie Renton, a 57-year-old woman with a chronic anxiety state. She lives alone and is unemployed and her only interest is bingo. She is on a maintenance dose of diazepam, which is no longer helping. She finds it increasingly difficult to cope. What issues are to be covered at this consultation?

3.4 William Foulkes is an 18-year-old unemployed person who has fallen out with his parents regarding his contributions to the family home. He has nowhere to stay and seeks your advice on this. How would you handle this consultation?

3.5 Your next patient is Wilma Kemp, who lives with her 80-year-old mother, who is suffering with dementia. She feels that her mother cannot be left during the day while she is at work and asks how she can cope with this. Her job as a secretary is essential to survive. How would you manage this situation?

3.6 Mrs Sloan calls to see you. Her child, Vicki, aged 21 months, was seen by you 2 days previously and the mother was reassured that the child was suffering from flu-like symptoms. Vicki developed vomiting after the consultation and was sleepy. She was seen by one of the partners, who referred her to hospital. The mother informs you that

Vicki is in hospital and has insulin-dependent DM. Outline how you would handle this consultation.

3.7 Joseph Smith, a 28-year-old office-worker, suffers from MS. His condition is progressive and he visits you to request new therapy which he has read about in the popular press, namely an interferon-like product. This has been reported as a major breakthrough. How would you handle this consultation?

3.8 Your next patient is Jennifer Smith, a 7-year-old asthmatic child who is reasonably well controlled on her therapy. However, she is a consistent bedwetter and her mother demands that something is done about this. Jennifer is the oldest of five children. Her father is unemployed and they live in a deprived area. Discuss how you would handle this consultation.

3.9 Your next patient is a 42-year-old, Amanda Oliver, who suffers from Down's syndrome. Her mother, who was a single parent, died last year. She now lives with an uncle. She attends a centre for the disabled and has recurrent symptoms of UTI. How would you handle this situation?

3.10 Your next patient, Michael Smith, is a 71-year-old retired miner who has COAD. He refuses to take regular therapy but receives intermittent antibiotics. He is a heavy drinker and smokes 30 a day. His main complaint is of his progressive breathlessness. How would you manage the situation?

MEQ 4

4.1 David Black is a 40-year-old unemployed joiner who has had a drink problem for the last 10 years. Despite being a regular attender at surgery, he rarely takes any advice given, but is now worried as he has developed a tremor. What issues are presented at this consultation?

4.2 Your next patient is Stephen Hastie, a 43-year-old schoolteacher. He has a 2-week history of increasing central chest pain which is related to exercise. The longest the pain has lasted is 20 minutes. He smokes 20 cigarettes per day and his father died of coronary thrombosis when aged 40. Discuss your management of this situation.

4.3 Your next patient is Katy Jones, who is a 30-year-old secretary. She lives with her 34-year-old partner, who is a computer operator. She noticed a breast lump last night and is extremely worried. How would you manage this situation?

4.4 Your next patient is Donald Murphy, a 68-year-old who has recently been attending the urology clinic. He lives with his 70-year-old wife, who is crippled with arthritis. He tells you that prostatic cancer has been diagnosed and that a letter is being sent to you. Discuss the issues which require discussion at this consultation.

4.5 Your next patient is a 72-year-old, Michael Watt, whose wife died 4 weeks previously. He lives alone, although a daughter lives nearby. He has symptoms which are suggestive of depression. What are the important issues to be discussed at this consultation?

4.6 Your next patient is Maria Quigley, a 43-year-old housewife, who is distraught, having learned that her husband is having an affair. She consults about once annually and has no past history of note. She has two children, both of whom are away from home studying at university. How would you handle this consultation?

4.7 Irene Campbell, a 45-year-old, whom you have not seen for some time, requests HRT. She is an accountant and is unmarried. What issues arise and how would you handle this consultation?

4.8 Jason Campbell is a 24-year-old van-driver. He has been married for 5 years and has three children. He has been having recurrent dyspepsia for the last month. He admits to some difficulties making ends meet. What issues do you wish to cover at the consultation?

4.9 Jim and Jean Blair are in their late 30s, both lawyers. They have decided that they would like to start a family and have made the appointment to discuss the genetic risks attached to this. How would you handle this consultation?

4.10 Mary Fegan is aged 43 and a frequent attender at the surgery. She has long abused alcohol and suffers from short-term memory loss and poor decision-making. She has been unemployed for 3 years and has changed house three times in the past year. She calls asking for a tranquillizer as life events are getting on top of her. How would you handle this consultation?

MEQ 5

5.1 It is Monday morning and your first patient is John, aged 54. He is fat and a smoker and has known IHD, as do his two brothers. He comes to ask you if it is worth his while applying for a Large Goods Vehicle (LGV) licence. Outline your response.

5.2 At the end of the consultation, while he is there, John wonders if you can help him with his toe. Removing his shoe and sock you find that his left great toe is swollen and purulent and has a nail that is cut back 'hard'. What is your diagnosis and how would you manage this consultation?

5.3 Your next patient is Fiona. She is 60 and complains of cystitis. She has burning, dysuria and frequency. Outline your consultation.

5.4 Thomas, who is 50, has had recurrent indigestion for most of the time that you have known him. In 1972 he had a barium meal, which showed he had a DU. He wants the new tablets his friend has got. What would you wish to cover in the consultation?

5.5 Jim attends for his routine prescription review. He has had asthma for some years. He works as a binman and is quite happy with the way things are going. Reviewing his prescription you note that he uses lots of salbutamol inhalers but rarely orders his steroid inhaler. Proceed.

5.6 A very frightened Ann comes in next. She is 18 and after blushing tells you she has a sore ear. Examination reveals no abnormality. What thoughts go through your mind?

5.7 She smiles at you after your explanation and tells you that she would like to go on the pill. She is social class 5, gets an occasional migraine attack and has been sexually active since she was 16.

5.8 Jimmy is a rare attender. He comes in and asks for a sick note because he has to stay at home for a couple of weeks to look after his elderly mother. How do you respond?

5.9 Margaret is depressed. She has been seeing you for some weeks. Her marriage is breaking down and she is the 'guilty party'. She is not improving. She asks, 'What should I do, doctor?' Outline your response.

5.10 Your surgery is interrupted by Betty Bloggs, a social worker, who has rung up and would like you to tell her about Susan Jones, one of your patients, who has ME. Proceed.

MEQ 6

6.1 Damian is a drug addict and is known to be violent. He attends without an appointment. How do you manage this situation?

6.2 Damian wants 'a few temazepam' and seems to be under the influence of drugs. How do you proceed?

6.3 Your next patient is Beverley, a sweet little girl of 3 who makes her mother's life a misery by never sleeping at night. How do you manage this consultation?

6.4 Alice rings you during surgery. She is pregnant for the second time and it is 14 weeks since her last period. She tells you that she has had a show of blood. How would you proceed?

6.5 Mrs Lacey brings Natalie, who is 3. She wonders if she is getting migraine like her dad. She is hot and full of cold and complaining of a headache. Outline how you would proceed.

6.6 Your practice manager pops in to tell you that a patient wishes to complain about the practice assistant's management of his son. How would you deal with this situation?

6.7 Your investigation revealed, thankfully, that there had merely been a misunderstanding between the patient and the doctor and the problem is solved with informal discussion. You note, however, when reviewing the doctor's record of the case that he has been giving an 8-year-old child soluble aspirin. What are the implications of this?

6.8 Your next patient is Donald. He is a new patient who tells you he is having treatment for his prostate from his previous doctor. Reviewing his notes, you find that he is receiving pharmacological treatment for prostatism without having had any baseline investigation of his blood or urological examinations. What are the implications for you in this consultation?

6.9 The next patient is Susan Jones, your patient with ME. She is very angry because no one takes her seriously and she feels so unwell. Proceed.

6.10 She is seeing a doctor in a town some miles away for gamma globulin injections. She asks you if she should continue seeing him. How do you respond?

MEQ 7

7.1 Your first patient, Michael Stuart, age 16, presents with a sore throat. He says his mother has sent him to get an antibiotic because he has some important examinations coming up. Describe with reasons your response and your management of Michael.

7.2 The next patient is a postgraduate student from Iran, age 23, who has just registered with the practice. He has been troubled by frequent, loose motions five to six times a day for the last 3 weeks. He has not had similar symptoms before. He feels unwell and admits he is finding his new course very stressful. How would you manage this consultation?

7.3 Your next patient should have been Pam David, age 50. She attended the previous evening with a lump in her neck and you found marked lymphadenopathy. You invited her back for further tests. She fails to attend. How would you respond to this situation?

7.4 John Peter is a 40-year-old self-employed decorator. He attends with a 3-day history of back pain. He says he has been resting but the pain has not improved. He asks if you could recommend a good chiropractor. How would you respond?

7.5 Anne Cane is aged 28 and the mother of four children. Her husband had a vasectomy 3 years ago. She presented with a 3-month history of amenorrhoea, but insisted that she had not had any other partners. A pregnancy test has now been reported as positive. Describe your approach.

7.6 Ellen Tudor brings in her 6-year-old child, Sophie. Sophie has been diagnosed as having 'glue ear'. The mother says that the local hospital has told her the child should be admitted for insertion of grommets, but there is a 6-month waiting-list. She ask your advice as to whether she should go privately. Discuss the factors you would consider in your reply.

7.7 You took a smear from Diana Platt, a student of 19. This has been reported as being unsatisfactory and showing Trichomonas. Diana's mother telephones to say that Diana has now gone to France for a year and has asked her to ring for the result of the smear. How would you manage this conversation?

7.8 A visit is made to a man of 74 with angina. He tells you his wife is due to be discharged from hospital following a stroke. Apparently she still has considerable difficulty in walking and finds it hard to get the right words on occasion. He is very worried about his ability to cope. Discuss how you would plan the continuing care of this couple.

7.9 One partner suggests that there is an increased amount of violence in the practice area and they are no longer happy about doing evening or weekend visits to certain parts of the practice unaccompanied. Discuss the issues facing the practice.

7.10 A brainstorm of the practice staff was carried out to decide on the next round of practice audit activity. The following list was produced. Choose three items and give brief arguments for their inclusion.
- Alcohol problems.
- Accessibility of the surgery to the disabled.
- Acne.
- Benign prostatic hyperplasia.
- Influenza vaccination.
- Repeat prescription procedures.
- The red eye.
- Vaginal discharge.

MEQ 8

8.1 Your first patient, Stephen Owen, a medical student of 24, presents with a painful rash on the left buttock. It has been present for 3 days. You diagnose herpes zoster. He tells you that he had thought this was possible and asks whether antiviral creams or tablets would help him. Discuss your response.

8.2 Your next patient, Peter Abel, requests PCP for his girlfriend. He says that a condom failed the previous night, but she is too embarrassed to attend herself. Discuss, with reasons, how you would respond.

8.3 The next patient is Lachmi Singh, a 62-year-old woman with DM. She comes with her daughter, who requests a repeat prescription of glibenclamide and paracetamol. You note that Mrs Singh has not had blood (including HbA_1C) checked for 15 months. She did not respond to an invitation to attend the practice diabetic miniclinic. How might you manage this situation?

8.4 Your next patient is Roger Dane, age 56. He has been to see a gastroenterologist because of persistent abdominal discomfort. He brings a handwritten note from the consultant asking you to prescribe a new drug and giving the name of the supplier. You have not heard of this drug and there is no information in the *BNF*. What dilemmas does this request confront you with and how might they be resolved?

8.5 During the surgery the receptionist asks you to speak to Dermot Stephens, who is requesting an urgent call on the telephone. This 70-year-old man suffers from acute panic attacks, but also has known COAD and IHD. He has already had three emergency calls this week because he says he is breathless. Discuss the options available to you in the management of this man.

8.6 After surgery the practice manager says that there has been trouble at reception because a patient was demanding an appointment that day and all the appointments were full. Discuss the roles of different members of the PHCT in producing an answer to this problem.

8.7 There is a request for a visit to Naomi Root, age 23. She is 9 weeks pregnant and bleeding vaginally. She lost a previous pregnancy at 12 weeks. Discuss your management of this situation.

8.8 At the practice meeting it is intended to discuss the appointment of new staff. One partner is very keen to employ a counsellor. Another partner would like an extra practice nurse to develop chronic disease clinics. Discuss the factors that should be considered in the decision.

8.9 The practice manager tells you that during the year the cost of deputizing service use has risen by 50%. Discuss the implications of this statement.

8.10 Below are listed the five key areas from the Health of the Nation strategy. Choose three and write brief targets for a practice policy to address them.
- Coronary heart disease and stroke.
- Cancers.
- Mental illness.
- HIV/AIDS.
- Accidents.

MEQ 9

9.1 Michelle Moore, a 13-year-old girl, attends your morning surgery. She tells you that she is concerned because her periods are infrequent (every 10 weeks) and painful. You notice in the records that she saw a partner in the practice with the same complaint 1 month ago and had a pregnancy test carried out, which was negative. What issues are raised by this consultation?

9.2 During your coffee break you receive a phone call from Kate Campbell, a friend who is not a patient. She tells you she is about to go on holiday to Tanzania, and asks if you could supply her with some ciprofloxacin for use if she develops infective diarrhoea. How might you respond?

9.3 Your next patient, Ian Ferguson, is a man aged 55 who normally works as a gardener. He has been off work for several weeks after a wrist fracture, which is still causing him some pain. It seems unlikely that he will be able to return to operating heavy machinery. He asks you if you would support his request for early retirement on health grounds. How would you respond?

9.4 Your next patient, Sarah Spencer, is a woman of 45 who consults you regularly about an anxiety state. On this occasion she tells you that something she worries about a lot is that her mother died of Huntington's chorea. How would you advise her?

9.5 At coffee time you are visited by a representative from a pharmaceutical company who asks if you would like to attend a scientific meeting in Nice. Your expenses would be reimbursed. The meeting appears to be legitimate and the subject interests you. What issues does this invitation raise?

9.6 A 35-year-old schoolteacher, Paul Wright, presents with a 4-day history of cough, wheeze and copious green sputum. There is no significant past history and on examination he has expiratory rhonchi but no signs of consolidation. Outline and explain your management.

9.7 Naomi Moss, a 25-year-old hairdresser, asks for a supply of acyclovir cream, to treat recurrent cold sores. How would you respond?

9.8 After surgery you visit Andy Smith, a 56-year-old man you recently referred to the chest physicians. He has been discharged after investigation with a diagnosis of terminal bronchogenic carcinoma. Mrs Smith asks to speak to you alone for a moment. She tells you that Andy does not know the diagnosis and she asks you not to tell him the truth as it would surely kill him. How would you respond?

9.9 Harry Jones, a 19-year-old student, presents on his return from spending a year-out backpacking in the Far East. He complains of weight loss and general malaise. What possible problems might account for this and what initial investigations would you carry out?

9.10 Your long-serving practice manager tells you that she intends to retire in 3 months. The partners decide that you should draw up a 'person profile' of the appropriate replacement. Outline the features that would make up the profile of a practice manager.

MEQ 10

10.1 Just before you are due to start morning surgery, you are asked to see Calum Davidson, a 46-year-old man who has presented at reception with chest pain. From the history it becomes clear that Mr Davidson is having an MI. Outline your management.

10.2 Your first booked patient of the day is Mrs Jane Stone, a 73-year-old widow. She tells you that, on the advice of her son, a physician in the USA, she has come for a cholesterol check. How would you respond?

10.3 Your next patient is 7-year-old Tom Turner, who attends with his mother, Sharon, for a routine review of his asthma. He is currently using salbutamol via a large-volume spacer device as needed. What criteria would you use to decide on further management?

10.4 Your next patient is George Hagan, a 52-year-old bank clerk, who is attending as a result of a new-patient medical, at which your practice nurse measured his blood pressure at 146/104. There is no significant past or current history. Outline your management plan.

10.5 At coffee time your practice manager mentions that the staff were concerned that your first patient, Mr Davidson, had looked quite unwell in the waiting-room. The staff members felt they would not have known what to do if he had collapsed. What issues does this raise for the practice?

10.6 Your next patient is Jane Hepburn, a 34-year-old woman, who complains of a sore face. When you examine her, it becomes clear that the cause is a carious tooth with a large cavity. Mrs Hepburn readily agrees with this diagnosis and tells you that she has come to you rather than the dentist because the dentist wants £30 to see her. Outline your management.

10.7 Your next patient, 19-year-old Audrey Fonda, bursts into tears when she enters the room. When she calms down, she tells you that she has just broken off her engagement and wishes to cancel her honeymoon trip due in 5 months' time. The travel agent has told her she will lose her deposit unless she can obtain a letter from her doctor to enable her to cancel on medical grounds. How would you handle this request?

10.8 Your next patient is Kurt Conham, a 25-year-old man, whom you know to have a long history of substance abuse. He brings a letter from the local drug abuse centre which asks you to prescribe long-term methadone. The letter is signed by a 'counsellor'. Discuss the implications of this request.

10.9 Your next patient, Diana Ferguson, who is a cook, attends for review after an episode of gastroenteritis. She was first seen by a partner in the practice 2 weeks ago. After a swab apparently grew *Helicobacter*, she was advised to stay off work until a negative specimen was obtained. Her second specimen is negative but, while telling her this, you notice that her first specimen was also negative; the *Helicobacter* swab related to a previous episode. What would you do?

10.10 Your prescribing adviser points out that your practice is spending a lot on ranitidine. The practice commissions you to produce a plan to reduce this spending. Discuss how you might make savings.

MEQ 11

11.1 You receive a message from a local gynaecologist informing you that Michaela Kelly, who is 11 weeks postpartum, was admitted the previous night by the deputizing doctor with heavy vaginal bleeding. She was discharged within 24 hours but her scan result is now to hand and shows a large vascular cystic area in the uterus, aetiology unknown. Under no circumstances should she have a D and C if further bleeding occurs. How would you respond to this?

11.2 Andrina Morrison is a 35-year-old woman who suffers from MS. She has recently read about the use of interferon in this disease and would like to know if, as a fundholding practice, you could prescribe this for her.

11.3 Nancy Nisbet is the elderly mother of one of your patients who has recently been diagnosed with breast cancer and bony secondaries. The mother is not your patient but she is keen to have more information about the diagnosis and prognosis as the family have given her no details and she wants to help to look after her daughter. How would you deal with this request?

11.4 Mary Burns comes with her 11-month-old daughter for the results of a second urine test which was requested by your partner. The previous MSSU was reported as showing enterococcal ? significance and the repeat test has given the same result. How would you proceed?

11.5 Mrs Deirdre Ferguson is a 64-year-old woman who joined your practice 1 year ago. She has had her new-patient interview with the practice nurse and saw one of your partners 6 months previously for a repeat prescription of Premarin (unconjugated oestrogen). This had been started by her previous general practitioner 12 years before. She is requesting a further 6-monthly prescription but, on questioning her, you discover that she has not had a hysterectomy. What issues does this raise?

11.6 A 17-year-old Asian girl, Brenda Prasad, requests the morning-after pill. She has had two similar consultations with other doctors in the practice. What areas would you like to cover?

11.7 Pauline McKay, an unmarried 37-year-old, has been coming to you with complaints of menorrhagia and severe dysmenorrhoea. She has been fully investigated by a gynaecologist, who has found no abnormality but has advised hysterectomy. She has appeared with her mother to discuss this with you. How would you proceed?

11.8 Gordon White is a 33-year-old infrequent attender who complains of intermittent weakness in his arms over the last few months. Recently he has dropped things on one or two occasions and thinks he may be stressed at work. How would you deal with this complaint?

11.9 Gary McQueen, 33, asks for a 1-week course of Nizoral tablets. He had a similar prescription 3 weeks ago but claims the chemist only had enough to dispense a 5-day supply. His skin condition has not improved and, since it was not his fault that he failed to complete the first course, he is refusing to pay for this prescription and demands that either you or the chemist does so. How would you deal with this situation?

11.10 The final patient of the day is an emergency who complains of a painful eye. Your receptionist informs you that he had been in surgery earlier in the day demanding to be seen but the appointment given then had been unsuitable. He had gone to casualty but it had been too busy for him to wait and he has now appeared at the surgery once more. How would you deal with this man?

MEQ 12

12.1 Iona Smith brings her 10-year-old son Ian to the surgery with a small verruca on the sole of his foot. She asks for a letter excusing him from sports until it resolves. How would you deal with this?

12.2 Willie McCann telephones the surgery complaining of a sore throat for 2 days, not helped by aspirin gargles. He is going abroad that evening and is unable to come to the surgery. What action would you take?

12.3 The practice holds a meeting to discuss changing your out-of-hours cover from an extended rota with a neighbouring practice to using deputizing. What aspects must the practice consider?

12.4 Mrs Ashraf Patel, a 53-year-old frequent attender, telephones the surgery complaining of epigastric pain. She is given advice and 30 minutes later you are called urgently to the house as she has collapsed. On arrival you find Mrs Patel dead. What problems confront you?

12.5 Frances Black, 32, comes to you complaining of weight gain since starting Provera for menorrhagia. She requests a prescription for Tenuate Dospan, which her sister had been prescribed by her own doctor with great success. How do you respond to this?

12.6 Marlene Dempsey contacts the surgery requesting a prescription for her 4-year-old son John, who is 'chesty'. You manage to call her back later in the day with the intention of seeing the child at the surgery. Mrs Dempsey informs you that all is well as your health visitor called earlier with a prescription for Amoxil. What issues does this raise?

12.7 Maria Ross, a 28-year-old business executive, is 2 months postpartum. She is breast-feeding her first child and is concerned and upset because he vomits after every feed. How would you deal with this?

12.8 Your practice nurse decides that she would like to start a travel clinic in the surgery. What implications does this have for the practice?

12.9 Mrs Linda Thomson, 50, enters your surgery and bursts into tears. She has discovered that her husband has been having an affair with a younger woman. She has not slept for a week and is very distraught. How would you help her?

12.10 A 74-year-old anxious woman, Stella Hillis, who is a frequent attender, is visibly upset about a consultation 2 days before with a locum doctor, who she claims was rude and aggressive towards her. She wishes to complain but is afraid you will put her off your list if she does so. How would you respond to this?

MEQ 13

Assume you are in a suburban, five-partner practice which has a full complement of ancillary staff and is non-fundholding.

13.1 Roger Turner, a 42-year-old accountant, comes to see you requesting referral for homoeopathic treatment. He has been suffering from headaches for some time and has been fully investigated by your partner but no cause has been found. What factors might influence your decision regarding the suitability of referral?

13.2 Martha Owen, a 48-year-old teacher consults you with symptoms of flushing, night sweats and anxiety. She says her periods have become irregular and scanty over the past 6 months and insists that HRT would help her. What factors would influence your response to her request?

13.3 The personnel officer of a local TV company (to whom you are medical adviser) phones you to ask for advice about the content of first-aid kits to be carried in company cars. What advice would you give?

13.4 One of your partners suggests that the practice opens a Sunday surgery to relieve the on-call work at weekends. What issues does this raise?

13.5 Mrs Higginson brings her 5-year-old daughter, Harriet, to you. She is very worried because she saw some droplets of blood on Harriet's pants last night. What issues might this consultation raise?

13.6 Mrs Driscoll attends surgery to tell you that she thinks she is pregnant. She is 38 and this is her first pregnancy. She has been on phenytoin to control her grand-mal seizures for some years. What advice would you want to give her?

13.7 Miss Powell, an 85-year-old woman with cataracts, attends your surgery for the third time in 3 months requesting that her admission for cataract surgery be expedited. She asks if she would be better off in a fundholding practice. What issues does this raise?

13.8 Mrs Falconer, a 30-year-old teacher, consults you saying that she is tired all the time. She is a new patient to your practice. She tells you that her previous doctor thought that she had ME and that she requires renewal of her long-term certification. On examination you cannot detect any physical abnormalities. She tells you that she has been fully investigated in the past but nothing has been found to be wrong. What factors would be relevant in this consultation?

13.9 Mr Barnes, a 35-year-old university lecturer, normally consults your senior partner who is currently on holiday. Your receptionist asks you what she should do about his request for a prescription for amoxycillin, which he says your partner always gives him when he has a cold. He is too busy to come to surgery and say that your partner never asks to see him when he requests such a prescription. He has no relevant past medical history. What issues are raised by this request?

13.10 Mrs Craig, the niece of an 80-year-old patient of yours, who is suffering with mild dementia, comes to surgery to discuss her aunt's future care. She says her aunt is not looking after herself properly but adamantly refuses to leave her own home. What issues might you wish to consider in this consultation?

MEQ 14

Assume you are in a suburban, five-partner practice which has a full complement of ancillary staff and is non-fundholding.

14.1 Mrs Norman is a 32-year-old married woman who came to see you last week complaining of a 3-week history of lower abdominal pain and vaginal discharge. Clinical examination suggested a diagnosis of pelvic inflammatory disease and the tests you performed are positive for gonorrhoea and *Chlamydia*. She returns today for the results of the tests. What would be your aims for this consultation?

14.2 Jean (28) has been trying to get pregnant since she married Brian (30) 3 years ago. Both are fit and well. As a preliminary investigation, you have arranged a sperm test for Brian. This shows a very low viable sperm count. The couple have returned today for the result. What would your aims be for this consultation?

14.3 Joan Dawkins, a 15-year-old, comes with her mother complaining that she is tired all the time. You cannot detect any physical abnormality and she denies any worries. After Joan leaves, Mrs Dawkins returns to tell you in confidence that Joan has missed her last two periods. She is worried that she may be pregnant. What issues does this consultation raise?

14.4 George Westlake, a 55-year-old builder, is a diabetic. He was diagnosed 5 years ago and has always had blood sugars of 12–15 mmol/litre. He tells you that he has stopped taking his 5 mg glibenclamide tablets because he feels better without them. What issues does this raise and how can they be resolved?

14.5 Rosemary is a fit 20-year-old who has been on the combined oral contraceptive pill for 3 months. When she attends for a routine pill check, she tells you that she has lost all interest in sex. How might you be able to help?

14.6 Florence Matthews, a 34-year-old waitress, consults you because she has aching legs. On examination, she has mild, bilateral, below-knee varicose veins. You cannot detect any other abnormality. She asks you to sign her off 'on the sick' until she has them treated at the hospital. You know that the waiting-list at the hospital is over 6 months. Describe your response to her request.

14.7 Wilhelmina Lloyd, a 50-year-old shop assistant, had a hysterectomy 3 months ago. She consults you for the seventh time this month with vague symptoms of malaise. You have fully examined and investigated her but cannot find any cause for her symptoms. What are the possible causes for her behaviour pattern and what can you do to help her?

14.8 Mary Walsh brings her 10-month-old son, Bertram, to see you as an emergency at the end of morning surgery. She tells you that he has been wheezing all night and asks whether this is asthma and if he should be admitted to hospital. What factors would you rely on to determine whether or not Bertram should be admitted to hospital?

14.9 You discover that the number of house calls you are doing has increased dramatically lately. Why might this be?

14.10 Your senior partner asks you to consider a letter she has had from a local girls' boarding-school asking her to be their medical officer. She is keen to accept. What issues would you need to discuss in relation to this topic?

MEQ 15

15.1 The first patient in surgery is a 16-year-old boy, Stuart Gray, who has a 48-hour history of a sore throat and unremarkable findings on examination. Discuss your options for concluding this consultation.

15.2 The next patient is a 46-year-old self-employed builder, John Collins, who was admitted to hospital 1 month ago with his first seizure. (Investigations at hospital since then have revealed no abnormalities but he has come to you to discuss his management.) How do you deal with important issues?

15.3 The next patient, Sandra Miller, is a 74-year-old woman who complains of a 3–6-month history of difficulty sleeping. What are the possible underlying causes?

15.4 A 6-year-old boy, David Kyle, is brought in by his parents. They found him playing with needles and syringes in a park. What are the immediate issues to be confronted?

15.5 The next patient is a 15-month-old girl, Angela Wilson, whose height and weight are below the third centile. On reviewing the notes it seems the child was normal at birth. Her failure to thrive has been worsening over the past 6 months. What features of the child's history would help you to define the cause?

15.6 You start to sign the repeat prescriptions after surgery. What are the criteria by which you would judge the adequacy of a repeat prescribing system?

15.7 While you are signing the repeat prescriptions, the mother of the 16-year-old boy in case 15.1 phones to ask why you did not give him the antibiotic which he normally gets. What issues does this raise?

15.8 You next visit a 68-year-old man, James Black, at home: he is dying of lung cancer. What areas of care do you wish to address at such a preplanned terminal-care visit?

15.9 At the evening practice meeting you discuss the Royal College of General Practitioners Diabetes Guidelines Pack and you are asked to prepare a protocol from this. How do you proceed?

15.10 You decide to carry out an audit of satisfaction with the services your practice offers. Which dimensions should you study?

MEQ 16

16.1 When you arrive for morning surgery you find a 7-year-old, Alison Burke, with her father in the treatment room. She sustained a 5 cm laceration to her forehead the previous day. What are the implications of this presentation?

16.2 Jane Smith, a 17-year-old girl, presents next, requesting the morning-after pill. What are the important ethical and practice management aspects of this consultation *vis-à-vis* patient autonomy?

16.3 Alex Thomson comes in next, a 48-year-old man who has been thrown out of the flat he shares with two other men because of his disruptive behaviour most evenings, when intoxicated. How do you assess his problem and what help can you offer him?

16.4 James Morton, your next patient, is a 74-year-old retired miner who was bereaved a year ago. He is currently experiencing back pain, headaches, constipation and insomnia. The main physical findings are the non-verbal cues, which suggest depressed mood. What difficulties might you experience in communicating a diagnosis of depression to this patient?

16.5 A 37-year-old married university lecturer, whose family you know very well, comes requesting the OCP. Her husband had a vasectomy 2 years ago, after the birth of their third child. What are the implications of this request?

16.6 Dennis McDaid, a 27-year-old temporary resident, is next. He requests a prescription for oral methadone. What are the implications of this?

16.7 Ann Stewart is a 27-year-old personal secretary who has just discovered she is pregnant. She asks you about the precautions she should take before going on holiday to Kenya for 6 weeks. What is your response?

16.8 A 46-year-old man, John Smith, then visits complaining of impotence. He says he wants to take the pills your partner gave him 20 years ago for the same thing. How might you be able to help?

16.9 John Brown, a 46-year-old businessman, comes in requesting a sickness certificate because of increasing business pressure due to debt. He reminds you that he had a 'possible MI' 3 years ago. How do you respond and what implications might this have for your future relationship with the patient?

16.10 Alan James is a 33-year-old electrical engineer with a non-specific chest pain today for the first time. He has no risk factors for IHD. What can you do to minimize the possibility of somatic fixation?

MEQ 17

You are one of six partners in a group practice working from a purpose-built surgery. The partnership operates a personal list system whenever possible and has a 10-minute appointment system.

17.1 Your first patient is Tracy Bell, aged 21. She works at the checkout counter in a local food supermarket. Tracy tells you that she has read in a woman's magazine about 'Norplant' and asks if you could provide her with this means of contraception. What information should be provided for Tracy and how might a decision about this treatment be achieved?

17.2 Having just completed the consultation with Tracy Bell, you are interrupted by a phone call from a local hotel. Apparently a visitor from North America, Mr Canyon, aged 64, has requested an urgent visit on account of the very recent onset of severe chest pain. Outline your likely strategy for dealing with such a situation (excluding the acute clinical assessment and management of his chest pain).

17.3 You return to your surgery 1 hour later. Your patients have all rebooked at a later time, extending the length of your surgery. The next patient is a woman aged 50, who is a lawyer and the wife of a company director. She has come for a BP check and to renew her prescription for atenolol and temazepam. She enters your room in a fury, saying, 'This service is despicable; I thought there was a Patient's Charter.' How would you respond?

17.4 Your next patient, Mr Cyril Rollington, has just joined your practice. He informs you that he has recently been appointed as charge nurse in your local district general hospital. He tells you that he is HIV-positive but requests that the information be kept entirely confidential between you and him. What dilemmas does this present and how may they be resolved?

17.5 Your next patient is a 35-year-old married woman, Mrs Sandra Simpkins. She tells you that, despite trying to conceive for some 12 months, she has not yet become pregnant and asks if there is anything that should be done at this stage. (a) List the items of information you need to know before you answer her question. (b) What explanation would you give her about general management of failure to conceive?

17.6 Susan Springwell, aged 48, is terminally ill with carcinomatosis secondary to ovarian carcinoma. She is cared for by her husband Jack and an unmarried daughter Clare, aged 22. The district nurse speaks to you prior to a routine house visit, stating that, despite oral diamorphine, Mrs Springwell is in severe pain and extremely distressed. How can you help?

17.7 John Brown, a single, 25-year-old, truck-driver, consults you. He tells you that 2 years ago, while driving a large vehicle, he knocked down a cyclist, who subsequently died. He has recently had difficulty sleeping and has been unable to work for the past 2 weeks, saying that he is too fearful to drive to work. How can you help?

17.8 The senior partner of the practice is on holiday and you have been allocated a patient from his chronic visiting list. Mrs Cecilia Drummond-Smith is a wealthy widow aged 78, living in a large house. On arrival your first observation is that she seems to be extremely fit and well. From her sparsely written medical records you note that she had a 'funny turn' some 2 years previously but there have been no medical events since then and she is not on any medication. She greets you warmly and immediately pours you a glass of sherry. Outline your management of this situation.

17.9 After a busy day in the practice you are off duty and awakened at 2.00 a.m. by a telephone call. An acquaintance informs you that his son, aged 4, is desperately ill with an asthma attack and requests that you come at once. Outline the problems presented by this situation and how they may be resolved.

17.10 You are asked by the headmaster of a local comprehensive school to provide an afternoon of sexual health education to a mixed class of sixth-form boys and girls. Outline your proposed structure and content.

MEQ 18

18.1 Your first patient on a Monday morning is Sarah Simpson, aged 17. She requests the morning-after pill. You see from her records that there have been three similar requests over the past few months. How would you respond?

18.2 Mrs Robertson, aged 51, is your next patient. She has come at the behest of her husband as he feels she should have HRT, but she is not particularly keen. How can you help?

18.3 Your next patients are a couple who are about to proceed on their honeymoon to Kenya some 3 weeks hence. They say they have had all the appropriate vaccinations but request prescriptions for antimalarials. How do you respond?

18.4 In the middle of your morning surgery you receive a call from the mother of a 3-year-old child. She informs you that Billy has had diarrhoea for 2 days and is crying with abdominal pain. You decide to visit in 1 hour on completion of your morning surgery. When you arrive at the house you are informed by a neighbour that the mother dialled 999 and that the child is now on the way to hospital. What are the implications of this event?

18.5 Later that day you visit a patient living in the same street as Billy. The patient says, 'All the neighbours are furious because you refused to visit Billy.' (Billy was discharged without treatment following the emergency 999 call.) What do you do?

18.6 In surgery your next patient is Susan, a 15-year-old girl with Down's syndrome. She is accompanied by the officer-in-charge of the residential home where she lives. You are informed that Susan has been very sexually provocative and there is concern that she might become pregnant. It is requested that you arrange contraception in the form of Depo-provera by injection. How would you respond?

18.7 Your next patient is a 36-year-old woman. She has three children aged 5, 7 and 11 and is recently divorced. She informs you that she was sterilized after the third pregnancy. She is now living with a man aged 24 and they wish to have a child. She asks that you refer her for reversal of sterilization. What are the issues involved in such a request?

18.8 Present out-of-hours arrangements in your practice are that the duties are shared equally between all partners. You learn that a national deputizing service is offering its service to your practice and the youngest partner in the practice has, at the weekly practice meeting, asked that he be allowed to use this service. What are the implications of this request?

18.9 Your next patient is a 9-year-old girl, Patricia. Her mother has brought her to see you following a recent hospital admission, when it was diagnosed that Patricia has diabetes. Speculate on the future events in the life of Patricia.

18.10 Your practice receives a letter from the medical director of your FHSA/health board in which you are informed that prescriptions for drugs acting on the respiratory system for your practice cost 25% above the national average. What action should you take?

MEQ 19

19.1 Mr Harry Hughes, aged 54, comes to see you in morning surgery. He has been on atenolol 50 mg a day for 2 years for control of his BP. His BP on treatment has been satisfactory. Today he throws his atenolol pill on the desk and declares that he is fed up with taking your pills; he is going to try homoeopathy. What factors should you consider in trying to resolve this situation?

19.2 Mrs Kay Kettering, a 52-year-old divorcee, attends to enquire about HRT. She tells you that she has read that it is good for one's sex life. What areas do you cover in this consultation?

19.3 Debbie Drake, aged 15, attends your surgery unaccompanied. She looks embarrassed, and asks if she can have the morning-after pill. Discuss your management.

19.4 Your next patient is Mr Reginald Wright, who complains of recent onset of rectal bleeding. On rectal examination you feel a hard mass that you are fairly sure is malignant. He has no obvious clinical spread. How do you handle this situation?

19.5 At coffee time your health visitor suggests that the practice should start a 'quit smoking' group. How do you respond?

19.6 Your first visit is to a 35-year-old woman who is just home from hospital, having had a complete miscarriage at 10 weeks gestation in her first pregnancy. Your partner sent her in as an emergency two nights ago. What areas do you wish to cover on this visit?

19.7 You are contacted at 3.00 a.m. while on call for the practice by Mrs Shirley Collins. She wonders if you can pop out to see her 4-year-old daughter, Lucy, who has a temperature of 102°F. How do you respond?

19.8 Your PACT figures show that the practice is 30% above the FHSA average for respiratory drugs. Your fund manager suggests that you should make savings on these drugs. What areas do you cover in your discussion?

19.9 Your full-time female partner proposes at a partnership meeting that she would like to introduce personal lists in the practice. What areas should be covered in the ensuing discussion?

19.10 Your practice manager informs you that your ECG machine is beyond repair. It will cost £3000 to buy a new one. What would you expect to be discussed in the decision to replace it?

MEQ 20

20.1 A 50-year-old businessman, Ray Hunter, attends your surgery complaining of difficulty sleeping and of lethargy. He attributes it all to regular business trips to America. He wonders if you could just prescribe him a few sleeping pills. How would you hope to handle this consultation?

20.2 A 26-year-old secretary, Jill Hodges, comes to say that she has stopped taking the OCP because she and her husband wish to try for a child. She says that they want to do all the right things for a healthy pregnancy. What areas should be covered in the consultation?

20.3 Mrs Ellen Brown, a 42-year-old woman with frequent somatic symptoms, attends with a history of headaches for the past month. They appear to be tension headaches. She asks if she could pay for a private brain-scan; she is not insured. How would you hope to reach a satisfactory conclusion to this consultation?

20.4 You are in surgery when the receptionist interrupts your consultation with an urgent visit request. Mrs Brown is on the telephone worried about her 58-year-old husband, who has a history of angina; she asks if you could 'come quickly doctor, I'm sure he's having a heart attack'. What do you do?

20.5 In evening surgery Mr Alec Baldwin, a 35-year-old travelling salesman, comes to see you. You have been treating him over the past 3 weeks for a persisting chest infection which is slow to resolve with your treatment. Speculate on the reasons for his slow recovery.

20.6 Mr John Jefferies, a 31-year-old executive, comes along to ask for a vasectomy. He has been married for 7 years and has two children aged 2 and 4. How do you advise him?

20.7 Your next patient is Mrs Gladys Pound, who is recently bereaved. You looked after her husband, Maurice, at home for his last 3 months with carcinoma of the bronchus. He died peacefully 3 weeks ago. She says, 'I'm sorry to bother you, doctor, but I have a bit of a chesty cough.' How would you wish to carry out this consultation?

20.8 Your practice nurse asks if you could review your surgery's needlestick policy. What areas should you cover with her?

20.9 You receive a letter from a neighbouring general practitioner. She is organizing a co-operative locally to cover out-of-hours care and would like to know if you are interested in joining the co-op once it is set up. How do you respond?

20.10 You agree to give a talk to a small group of medical students on the subject of 'Why you should choose general practice as a career'. What do you wish to include in your talk?

THE ANSWERS

MEQ 1

Susan, aged 12, has cerebral palsy with severe dystonic tetraplegia following birth injury. She has had recurrent severe chest infections. In recent months swallowing has become so difficult and dangerous that she now has a gastrostomy tube by which means she is fed. She also has convulsions and requires anti-epileptic therapy. There are two younger children under school age in the family and the mother is separated from her husband. What are the management issues in her case?

CONSTRUCTS

1 Community care. Define help available, both from the practice with the practice team and the support from social workers. Will require to be throughout the day and could involve nights from time to time.

2 Mother's health. This is extremely important as she is the only adult in the house and will be under considerable stress. Breaks of several weeks at a time are important in the long-term care.

3 Family support. Important that family are supported by relatives, friends, neighbours and the caring professions.

4 Management within family context. This will be in the community within the family setting and all the support mechanisms will be used.

5 Care of Susan. Must be humane and with sensitivity, with what is best for Susan considered at all times.

6 Family expectations. These have to be realistic, both about themselves and about the services provided.

1.2

You are invited to give a talk to a mother-and-toddler group on the subject of child health. List the issues you would raise.

CONSTRUCTS

1 Child development. Explain normality and ranges of normality and how this is taken care of within paediatric surveillance. Emphasize that the mothers and health professions have a particular role to play in paediatric surveillance.

2 Communication. Emphasize the important role which the mothers play and, if they have any concern, who they should communicate with among the caring professions.

3 Normal physiology. Emphasize the large ranges of normality and how abnormality is uncommon in this age-group.

4 Sexual health issues. Although the talk is related to child health, the mothers' health, contraception and the mothers' well-being are important areas to mention.

5 Health education/prevention. The preventive measures within the surgery are carried out by the health visitor. This should be mentioned, together with the importance of the immunization programme.

1.3

Amanda, aged 3 months, normal birth weight and history, attends your clinic with her mother. The mother states that Amanda has had a constant cough, is always breathless and often has sputum. She frequently sneezes and appears to have a blocked nose. Her bowels are loose. On examination she is marasmic and has considerable respiratory distress, with many adventitious sounds in the chest. This is the first occasion you have met this child with her mother and no previous notes are available. You wish to explain matters to Amanda's mother. What points would you propose to discuss?

CONSTRUCTS

1 Mother's beliefs and expectations. What does the mother think the cause of the symptoms is? Why does she think Amanda continues to lose weight and is distressed? What does she hope to gain from the consultation?

2 Diagnostic possibilities. Infective origin. Feeding problem. Error of metabolism. Malabsorption problem. Congenital abnormality.

3 Management. Will require investigation both in the surgery and ? referral to paediatric out-patients. Treatment of immediate problem of blocked nose and respiratory distress would seem the most urgent.

4 Communication. Take careful history from mother, asking open questions and listening. Be aware of child abuse. However, be sensitive and caring.

5 Follow-up. This should be 48 to 72 hours to deal with immediate problem but then to work out a plan of action regarding investigating the other signs. Consider referral to paediatric out-patients.

1.4

Mr and Mrs Williams, aged 27, live in a large town which has a general and obstetric hospital. Mrs Williamson comes home from the obstetric hospital, having had her second child, Ian, birth weight 3.5 kg, normal delivery, aged 3 days. The midwife informs you that the baby is jaundiced. What issues does this present?

CONSTRUCTS

1 Aetiology. Likely to be a slow physiological process as child has been discharged. Likely that hospital will have excluded more serious causes but this should be checked with hospital.

2 Management. Both the general practitioner and midwife to visit on daily basis. Check on child's feeding and general condition. Mother to contact team if any concerns.

3 Role of hospital. This would be as backup if any problems arose with either the baby or Mrs Williamson. They would also check the bilirubin level if the jaundice persisted or worsened.

4 Management within family context. Important that mother and child are in their own environment and that any expertise can be provided there.

5 Social issues. Adequate family and neighbour backup for the mother throughout the day as husband is likely to be at work.

6 Follow-up. Initially on a daily basis from both the doctor and the midwife, with doctor taking a lesser role as time passes. Postnatal examination and contraception remembered within that.

1.5

A brother and sister, John and Emma, aged 4 and 6, are brought up to you by their anxious mother. She is on holiday visiting elderly grandparents. She reports that the children have spots on their hands and feet and the perianal area. The mother demands to know what is wrong. How would you progress?

CONSTRUCTS

1 Communication skills. Ask open questions and deal with anxiety. Are there factors other than the children's spots, e.g. elderly grandparents and problems at home?

2 Diagnostic skills. Take careful history and place this in the context of the physical findings.

3 Patient's beliefs. What does mother think could be the cause and does she think this could be serious?

4 Management. Reassure mother and children, unlikely to be anything serious. Advise mother to remove any precipitating cause and provide therapy if necessary.

1.6

A schoolgirl, Sharon, aged 15, is brought to see you by two of her schoolmates in your capacity as school doctor. The schoolgirl has hidden the fact that she might be pregnant from everyone except her schoolmates, and she panicked when she developed a rash which seemed very like the description of German measles which had been discussed in class by the school nurse as part of an educational programme. All three girls are with you together in the surgery. What issues arise?

CONSTRUCTS

1 Ethical issues. Limit the people that this can be discussed with. First duty is to the patient and the problems of discussing with headmaster, other pupils and parents.

2 Medicolegal issues. Sharon is under age for intercourse. Have to make judgement regarding how to deal with this.

3 Preventive issues. Girls under 16 unlikely to be using effective contraception. Should rubella screening and immunization be carried out in the school at an earlier stage?

4 Patient autonomy and thoughts. What does Sharon feel about the respective risks? What does she consider as the appropriate way forward?

5 Diagnosis and management. Establish whether Sharon has German measles by carrying out the appropriate titres and check whether she is pregnant. If both are positive, will require prophylaxis (gamma globulin) and close monitoring. Consider immunization programme for other girls.

1.7

Rupert, aged 12, is brought to see you by his mother, who is a lecturer in genetics. He is refusing to play rugby because he says his back is persistently sore. Rupert's mother reminds you that her daughter developed scoliosis, which was not recognized at an early stage. How would you proceed?

CONSTRUCTS

1 Family dynamics. Assess tensions within family, mother and daughter. What role does each have in the symptomatology?

2 Social issues. Mother has career. Does Rupert have necessary parental backup? Does he live at home? What are roles of father and other siblings?

3 Patient and mother expectations. Important to interview separately and assess what each wants from the consultation. Each is likely to have a different agenda.

4 Management. Take appropriate history. Arrange an X-ray if thought this would play an effective role.

5 Risk assessment. Weigh up the various conflicts. Be alert to the natural history of backache and take the appropriate action.

1.8

You live in a small town near a major paediatric hospital. Joseph, a boy of 12 years, attends you as an emergency. He has a deep knee laceration, and is reluctant to explain the origin. You know him well – he is fostered by your neighbours. You feel you could stitch the laceration but it is about the limit of your skills. The boy smells strongly of alcohol. What are the issues?

CONSTRUCTS

1 Ethical issues. Is Joseph doing something which he should not? Should you discuss with school, social work department, foster parents or inform the police?

2 Patient expectations. Does Joseph only want knee stitched or does he have some other issues which he wishes to discuss? Is it an appropriate time for that?

3 Communication issues. Be sensitive. Ask open questions. Look for clues of wider problems. Try not to be judgemental. Important to discuss alcohol abuse and widen this to other abuses. Cigarette and drug abuse. How do his peers feel about these matters?

4 Diagnostic possibilities. Smelling of alcohol. ? Other pathologies.

5 Management. Will be related to stitching his laceration and also discuss the wider issues already commented on.

1.9

The foster-parents suddenly arrive – both are clearly intoxicated. They state that the boy stole a motor scooter. The boy shouts that this is not true and viciously attacks his foster-parents. How would you handle the situation?

CONSTRUCTS

1 Family dynamics. Obvious tension between Joseph and the foster-parents. Assess situation as to who appears to be more reasonable. Consider help from those who have family skills, e.g. social work department.

2 Doctor's dilemma. Patient has to have priority but clearly as foster-parents are neighbours there are a number of conflicting forces.

3 Medicolegal. Problem of abuse. Joseph's history will be known to the social work department, as will the foster-parents. Important to involve them and also consider involvement of police as an offence has been committed.

4 Management within family context. This would be ideal but the situation may not lend itself to that. Could polarize situations but certainly explore as option.

5 Shelter. Joseph must have safe haven, and overnight in hospital until tempers have cooled would be one option. Other options could be considered, but the foster-parents' home would not seem sensible.

1.10

Your female trainee in the third week of her traineeship tells you that she is pregnant. Discuss the issues.

CONSTRUCTS

1 Interrupted trainee year. Lack of continuity within practice and in the continuing care of patients.

2 Education. This is designed for one uninterrupted year and would be affected.

3 Communication issues. Will clearly cause disruption to practice but try not to convey this to trainee, who is preparing for a major happy life event. Be empathic and interested.

4 Priorities. Emphasize the importance of training as a one-off situation and try not to deflect from that.

5 Partnership issues. Will cause some disruption to the practice: although the trainee is supernumerary, the practice gears its work to the trainee's presence. Try to get partners to take same priorities as trainer.

Commentary 1

This demonstrates the vast range of general practice, mainly at the younger end of the age distribution. It demonstrates the many skills and decisions required by the general practitioner, from health education, dealing with the normal, with varying degrees of normality, to dealing with the very abnormal. It illustrates how a rash can be very straightforward in one consultation and can have major implications in another. It illustrates a very difficult situation where patients are managed entirely in the community and the implications that this has for the community, in addition to the family and the practice. It includes a practical trainee problem. The constructs in this surgery include management of the patient and the family context, the range of community care and the social issues involved in sickness, with the importance of ethical and medicolegal matters.

MEQ 2

In your capacity as school medical officer to a primary school in a small town the headmaster asks you to see a young boy, John, just started school, aged 5, who is extremely disruptive in the classroom. He is being fostered with a view to adoption. The foster-mother has a full-time job as a social work administrator and the foster-father is based at home as a commercial artist and largely looks after the boy. The boy has been in the household for 6 months. How would you handle this situation?

CONSTRUCTS

1 Family dynamics. Relationship of boy to foster-mother and foster-father. How does he relate to any brothers and sisters and also to his family unit?

2 Social issues. Mother in social work and father working mainly at home. Experience as foster-parents. How does the boy relate in the classroom and relate to his parents?

3 Patient expectations. Is John aware that he is disruptive? Can he give any reasons for this and be part of any solution proposed?

4 Family expectations. Are foster-parents aware of disruption? What role can they play in the solution? Are they co-operative with the school?

5 Communication. Effectively with all those involved with John.

6 Confidentiality. All the professional groups involved in the discussion should be aware of their responsibilities.

7 Agreed plan. This should be formulated with the parents, with the school and with John. Could involve social work department, psychologist and, if persistent, child psychiatrist.

2.2

William, aged 6 years, is brought to see you by his mother. He has not been going to school for several weeks because the other children have been shouting 'smelly' at him because he had soiled pants. This is the first time you have met the mother and boy. List the information which you would wish to obtain before completion of the first consultation.

CONSTRUCTS

1 Family dynamics. Any problems at home: divorce, separation, illness, unhappiness, child abuse.

2 Social issues. Does he relate well to other children? Are there any learning difficulties, bullying? Does he enjoy school? ? Toilets at home and school.

3 Patient and mother expectations. What do they see as their own roles and the roles of the caring professions in the management? What do they see as the role of the school?

4 Communication issues. Take broad history, ask questions related to coping. Look for behavioural problems and any precipitating factor.

5 Diagnostic possibilities. Physical condition, e.g. CF, developmental delay, mental retardation.

6 Management issues. Should involve discussion with parents, teachers and health visitor and, if necessary, child guidance clinic.

2.3

You are asked to give general advice about dental hygiene for infants and preschool-age children. List the issues you would raise.

CONSTRUCTS

1 Communication issues. Be positive, stressing the importance. Outline the issues and be prepared to amplify if necessary.

2 Health education. Prevention better than cure. Importance of dental hygiene. Early attendance at dentist. Avoidance of sugar-containing feeds and snack foods. Benefit of fluoride.

3 Normal physiology. Outline the normal tooth development, both primary and secondary. Role of dietitian and patient understanding. Do parents realize the importance of health education and early attendance at the dentist?

4 Patient belief. Re-education regarding diet, e.g. snack foods and sugar-containing foods and emphasize value of all-round good nutrition.

2.4

Billy, aged 14, is brought to see you by his mother. He is a footballer of considerable quality and the next day is due to go on a special training camp for exceptional young footballers – an opportunity which will probably not arise again. He proves to have undoubted shingles (herpes zoster) of the left abdominal wall. The lesions have been appearing for about 2–3 days. List the issues in management of the condition.

CONSTRUCTS

1 Patient's expectations. As very important event, would probably expect very active therapy, e.g. acyclovir. Would expect fitness level to be unchanged.

2 Doctor's concerns. Regarding complications of herpes zoster, which could be accentuated by exercise. Also problem of infecting others.

3 Communication. Requires firmness, taking into account all the various factors. May require more directive approach.

4 Ownership of problem. Billy will minimize the problem, but he has to be part of its management.

5 Risk assessment. Weigh up the various factors and move forward accordingly.

6 Management plan. Arrange this, taking above into consideration.

2.5

A 37-year-old married woman, who is a teacher married to a dentist, attends your surgery because she thinks she may have become pregnant for the first time; she has been married for 7 years. She asks about the value of chorion villus sampling and, if she is pregnant, if this technique is helpful in assessment. Discuss the various problems presented.

CONSTRUCTS

1 Ethical issues. Requires honesty weighing up the various options. Mention higher risk of abortion with ? higher fetal abnormality but option of earlier termination.

2 Communication. Be positive and explain the importance of screening during pregnancy in her age-group.

3 Patient's beliefs and expectations. What has the patient heard about the technique and also the alternatives? Is she worried about being pregnant?

4 Patient autonomy. What does patient wish? Importance of her involvement in any decisions.

5 Health education. Importance of preventive measures during pregnancy, e.g. smoking, alcohol intake, exposure to infection.

6 Normal physiology. Present as normal process with available investigations; also discuss the pros and cons of blood screening, scanning, amniocentesis.

2.6

Ann, an only child, aged 14 years, is brought to see you by her father, who is divorced. He is a lorry-driver. For the past 6 weeks she has had a pain in her wrists, knees, shoulders and ankles. She feels nauseated and sweats at night excessively, and has not attended school. What are issues for the consultation?

CONSTRUCTS

1 Diagnosis and management. Unusual symptoms in 14-year-old. Requires blood investigations to exclude arthropathy or infective origin. Empathic approach and symptom relief will be main management issue.

2 Family dynamics. What support is there at home? Does she see mother or other brothers and sisters?

3 Social issues. Is father away from home? Who is responsible for her then? Performance at school? Relationship with peers?

4 Communication. Symptoms are worrying. Display a degree of concern but also that you are in control of the situation.

5 Follow-up. This is important. Should probably be after 1 week, or earlier if symptoms become worse.

2.7

In your capacity as general practitioner you see a 6-week-old infant, one of twins, with an illness that seems to be of a simple, viral, upper respiratory tract nature, very late in the evening. What are the issues?

CONSTRUCTS

1 **Diagnosis and management.** Careful history and examination. Unlikely to be any positive findings and parents likely to be reassured.

2 **Healh education.** Important to stress the mother's role. The importance of adequate food and sleep and the programe of immunization.

3 **Mother's expectations.** Is mother worried? What would she feel is an appropriate outcome? With twins, is she overawed by the work and the responsibility?

4 **Communication.** Explain management to mother. Take good history, using open questions.

2.8

Six hours later you are called suddenly by the mother, who says that the infant is dead in bed. You attend immediately and confirm that this is the case. Describe the actions required.

CONSTRUCTS

1 **Communication issues.** Listen, be sympathetic, discuss second twin and whether mother would like the child examined. Arrange assistance from family and neighbours.

2 **Mother's concerns.** Why was nothing picked up at previous visit? Why has this happened? Try to reassure, mention no warning of sudden infant death.

3 **Medicolegal issues.** Confirm death. Requirements for coroner, procurator fiscal. ? Autopsy. ? Inform police.

4 **Management.** Involve other members of practice team. Be empathic and sympathetic. Be aware of feelings of father. In long term, mention self-help groups.

2.9

At the end of the evening, when everybody else except the doctor has gone home and you still have four patients to see, the phone rings. It is Michael Sweeney, a 72-year-old retired miner, asking for advice about pains in his chest that have been coming and going for the past 2 to 3 days. How do you deal with this phone call?

CONSTRUCTS

1 Clinical safety. Possible diagnoses? Unstable angina, therefore an immediate visit to assess is required.

2 Patient expectations. Does he require immediate attention? Problem of consulting and patients waiting.

3 Other patients. Apologies should be given to other patients in the waiting-room, asking whether they would like to return the next day or wait until you return.

4 Other partners. One of these could be contacted to either go to the house or see the other patients in the surgery.

5 Practice organization. Steps taken in the event of an emergency should be clearly laid out in protocols.

2.10

Your trainee has been causing concern by being late for surgeries and unavailable when on call. You have discussed this with him and he denies there is a problem. What options are available in dealing with the problem?

CONSTRUCTS

1 Practice dynamics. Patients and staff inconvenienced. Will therefore add to the stresses within the practice.

2 Partner issues. With the patients and staff being inconvenienced, this will add stresses to the partnership and will add to an already difficult situation.

3 Licence to practice. Trainer required to sign that trainee has satisfactorily completed his training and this type of behaviour makes that very difficult. This concern must be conveyed to the trainee and others involved in his training.

4 Trainee opinion. Does he have any personal problems or problems at home? Is he ill, in debt, has he a drug problem or an alcohol problem?

5 Helping agencies. Within the trainer's support mechanisms either at trainee peer level, other trainers or those in the training hierarchy.

6 Risk assessment. Whether the trainee has the professionalism for independent practice.

Commentary 2

This surgery again has a wide range of problems, from pregnancy counselling to early diagnosis. It also illustrates the problem of the unexpected, with the sudden infant death. It illustrates the problem of patients being friends and also the difficulties when adequate professionalism is not reached. The constructs include family dynamics, normal physiology, communication and the problem of risk assessment. The surgery also illustrates decision-making when the patient and the doctor have completely different priorities.

MEQ 3

3.1

Jim Milroy is a 42-year-old rep. He has recently had a bronchoscopy which shows a bronchial carcinoma. He has arranged the consultation to discuss the outcome of the test. He attended as a day patient and is unaware of the result. However, he does admit to being worried. How would you handle this situation?

CONSTRUCTS

1 Communication and breaking bad news. Require empathy, listening and open questions. Be aware of the process of denial and guilt in coming to terms with the situation.

2 Patient autonomy. What are Jim's thoughts, both immediate and medium- and long-term? The effect on him, his family and work? What involvement does he wish to have in the decision-making?

3 Management options. Surgery, radiotherapy and chemotherapy. What is the place of each, the complications and the effects on outcome? What are the chances of a cure?

4 Social circumstances. Support at home and work, by both family and friends.

5 Patient's understanding. How much can be understood at this consultation? Empathic, with considerable patient involvement and adequate follow-up and backup arranged.

3.2

Fred Abbott is a 14-year-old who has been truanting from school. He calls without an appointment and demands to see you. He admits that he is addicted to heroin and wishes to be weaned off the drug. How would you manage the consultation?

CONSTRUCTS

1 Social circumstances. How independent is he? What support is there at home and from his family? Are they aware of the problem? Is there support at school and from the social services?

2 Practice dynamics. Are there many patients like this? Is there a practice policy for addicts? Do any of the partners or practice team have a special interest?

3 Reason for decision. Why has he decided now? Is he in trouble at home, at school or with the police? How committed is he to succeeding?

4 Management issues. How quickly can heroin be withdrawn? Does he require substitute? What support does he need at school, in the home and practice? Involvement of practice team and social services. Important that he realizes the problem is his.

5 Ethical issues. How much is known by family and school? Has he committed some crime and asked that school and police are not told? What can they be told in these circumstances?

3.3

Your next patient is Annie Renton, a 57-year-old woman with a chronic anxiety state. She lives alone and is unemployed and her only interest is bingo. She is on a maintenance dose of diazepam, which is no longer helping. She finds it increasingly difficult to cope. What issues are to be covered at this consultation?

CONSTRUCTS

1 Patient's ideas. What would she like regarding a successful outcome? What would her wishes be?

2 Patient's understanding. Does she recognize the various strands in the deprivation cycle? Does she see a link between her symptoms and circumstances?

3 Social circumstances. Does she have a support mechanism from family, neighbours, community, church, etc.? Can anything become positive rather than negative? From the support, who is available locally or more distant? What level of support can they provide? Could she have a holiday with them?

4 Management strategy. Describe role of patient, doctor, practice team, community. The role of counselling with drug problems and the clear definition regarding ownership of the problem.

3.4

William Foulkes is an 18-year-old unemployed person who has fallen out with his parents regarding his contributions to the family home. He has nowhere to stay and seeks your advice on this. How would you handle this consultation?

CONSTRUCTS

1 Family dynamics. Relationship with parents. Why so bad? Have there been recent precipitating factors, e.g. drugs or police? Any brothers or sisters? How do they fit in?

2 Social issues. Immediate problem of shelter; finance and caring agencies. Involvement of practice team and social work department. Any training prospects?

3 Peer group. Are friends in similar situation? Involvement with drugs/alcohol? Do they have outside interests? Financial? Employment situation?

4 Communication issues. Empathize with situation. Encourage communication with parents, caring agencies.

5 Patient's ideas. Does he realize he is different from the norm? What does he see as short-, medium- and long-term solutions? Does he realize that the problem is his?

6 Management issues. Backup of the practice team and also the social work agencies.

3.5

Your next patient is Wilma Kemp, who lives with her 80-year-old mother, who is suffering with dementia. She feels that her mother cannot be left during the day while she is at work and asks how she can cope with this. Her job as a secretary is essential to survive. How would you manage this situation?

CONSTRUCTS

1 Family dynamics. What help can be given to the family? Other support available, e.g. neighbours, relatives or friends locally?

2 Social issues. Safety of house. House functional for state of mother.

3 Management options. Day care for mother. Backup from the practice team and the social services. Attendance allowance. Help from neighbours. Care in the community and agreed plan for the way forward.

4 Work alternatives. Part-time work, flexitime, support of colleagues, early retirement.

5 Patient's point of view. What does mother think and how does that fit in with Wilma's opinion?

3.6

Mrs Sloan calls to see you. Her child, Vicki, aged 21 months, was seen by you 2 days previously and the mother was reassured that the child was suffering from flu-like symptoms. Vicki developed vomiting after the consultation and was sleepy. She was seen by one of the partners, who referred her to hospital. The mother informs you that Vicki is in hospital and has insulin-dependent DM. Outline how you would handle this consultation.

CONSTRUCTS

1 **Mother's point of view.** Facts from mother. Deal with anger or criticism. Empathize and explain difficulties.

2 **Medicolegal aspects.** Could be gathering facts to raise legal action. Important to empathize and communicate well. Listen and be prepared to clarify.

3 **Diagnosis of diabetes and what this means.** What has she been told at hospital? Effect on lifestyle. How condition is treated. Involve all members of family and support. Stress that development is normal.

4 **Social issues.** Mother will require support from general practitioner, hospital, practice team. Specific advice re-play, school, holidays, etc.

5 **Management.** For mother, family and child and will involve the general practitioner and hospital, support services and the practice team. The doctor has a dilemma regarding his future relationships with the family and whether they would be best dealt with by another doctor in the practice.

3.7

Joseph Smith, a 28-year-old office-worker, suffers from MS. His condition is progressive and he visits you to request new therapy which he has read about in the popular press, namely an interferon-like product. This has been reported as a major breakthrough. How would you handle this consultation?

CONSTRUCTS

1 **Patient autonomy.** What has he read and what hopes has this given? Difficulty because of remitting nature of the disease. Previous

products which have come to nothing. Progress of disease. How does he feel about condition? Does he feel it is progressive? How does he view the future?

2 Medicolegal aspects. Does he have a right to the treatment? Does it have considerable cost implications? Could there be legal challenge if he is not given that therapy?

3 Family involvement. Do others have an opinion about the treatment? Are they pressing for therapy? Have caring attitude, with hope, with caution. Involve the practice team and social services.

4 Care in the community. Could be useful in this situation and have an agreed way forward. Opinion of neurologist important.

5 Social issues. What support does he have at home?

3.8

Your next patient is Jennifer Smith, a 7-year-old asthmatic child who is reasonably well controlled on her therapy. However, she is a consistent bedwetter and her mother demands that something is done about this. Jennifer is the oldest of five children. Her father is unemployed and they live in a deprived area. Discuss how you would handle this consultation.

CONSTRUCTS

1 Family dynamics. How does she fit in? Father and mother's opinion. Family stress, e.g. housing and unemployment. Does the family have enough money, smoke too much, have too high an intake of alcohol?

2 Jennifer's thoughts. Is she concerned about bedwetting both at home and effect at school? The process upsets the family; does it upset her? Has Jennifer any role in management?

3 Social circumstances. In satisfactory housing, unemployment, little money? Anyway, does need backup to have washing-machine and drier if not already available. Important to be accepted at school and have the appropriate backup.

4 Course of condition. Likely to settle spontaneously, especially if no primary cause. Convey this information to mother and daughter.

5 Options for management. Manage in family context. Investigate star chart, MSU, IVP. Follow-up with encouragement and refer if thought to be necessary. Involvement of the practice team and the social support are invaluable in this situation.

3.9

Your next patient is a 42-year-old, Amanda Oliver, who suffers from Down's syndrome. Her mother, who was a single parent, died last year. She now lives with an uncle. She attends a centre for the disabled and has recurrent symptoms of UTI. How would you handle this situation?

CONSTRUCTS

1 Family dynamics. Role of neighbours and friends. Role of special school. Can you confide in someone there and give proper history? Assessment of capabilities. Can she live alone?

2 Social circumstances. Is uncle only option? Other relatives? ? Residential home for disabled, other interests, hobbies, social support. Aetiology of symptoms, infective, renal abnormality, diabetic, sexual abuse.

3 Management plan. Take proper history and investigate. Involve practice team and social work support. Treat infection.

4 Medicolegal aspects. If sexual or any other type of abuse, then involve the social work and practice team. Question of confidentiality.

5 Patient's understanding. Does Amanda know what's going on? What is her IQ and what are her thoughts regarding the management?

3.10

Your next patient, Michael Smith, is a 71-year-old retired miner who has COAD. He refuses to take regular therapy but receives intermittent antibiotics. He is a heavy drinker and smokes 30 a day. His main complaint is of his progressive breathlessness. How would you manage the situation?

CONSTRUCTS

1 Health promotion. Find out about smoking and drinking.

2 Social circumstances. Determine activities of peer group. Involvement at local pub.

3 Family dynamics. Is there anyone in the house to influence him or does everything revolve around him? His autonomy is important, with a definite role in this own management. Caring empathic approach but emphasize his important role.

4 Management plan. Involve Michael. Moderate exercise. Cut down drinking and stop smoking. Flu prevention. Antibiotics prophylactically. Is there a reversible component and should this be treated? Involve the practice team.

5 Care in the community. Should have some backup from this, with the relative risks of his various symptoms assessed and supported.

Commentary 3

The surgery, in addition to dealing with the diagnoses of serious conditions, also deals with the behavioural problems of bedwetting and drug abuse. There are also a number of social problems: the patient who has nowhere to stay and the large social element with the mother who has dementia. The difficulties in management of a non-remitting disease like MS are also covered and also the need for diagnosis in the early presentation of non-specific symptoms which can lead to a significant diagnosis (DM). The surgery also highlights the long-term problems with disability. The constructs in this surgery include breaking bad news, social issues, patient autonomy and the role of the special school. Some of these have been highlighted in previous problems but they do seem to be more prevalent at this surgery.

MEQ 4

David Black is a 40-year-old unemployed joiner who has had a drink problem for the last 10 years. Despite being a regular attender at surgery, he rarely takes any advice given, but is now worried as he has developed a tremor. What issues are presented at this consultation?

CONSTRUCTS

1 Health promotion. Now has symptom which could be related to alcohol intake and gives ideal opportunity. Although basically alcohol, widen to include exercise, smoking, diet, BP, etc.

2 Social circumstances. How does he fit in with his family, peer group, workmates? Does he have hobbies and what opportunity does he have for alcohol intake? Has there been a precipitating factor for symptoms, e.g. trouble with police?

3 Patient perception of medical care. What does he see as his role and the role of the doctor? Does he have any thoughts about autonomy, does he consider his condition to be medical in origin or social?

4 Diagnostic possibilities. Consider other causes.

5 Management of condition. This should look at the preventive measures and should include hobbies. There should also be a plan of investigation, with mention of the role of diet. In addition to the doctor, there will be involvement from the practice team and the social work department.

6 Communication issues. Communication should be empathic. The importance of the role of the patient should be stressed. The doctor should be caring and obtain information by open questioning.

7 Patient's understanding. Does he know there is a relationship between his symptoms and the intake of alcohol? Does he recognize his own role? Is he aware of the risks involved and what the likely outcome is of continuing to drink?

4.2

Your next patient is Stephen Hastie, a 43-year-old schoolteacher. He has a 2-week history of increasing central chest pain which is related to exercise. The longest the pain has lasted is 20 minutes. He smokes 20 cigarettes per day and his father died of coronary thrombosis when aged 40. Discuss your management of this situation.

CONSTRUCTS

1 Management of condition. The diagnosis is CHD until proved otherwise, and a series of investigations with appropriate medication should be commenced. If the angina is unstable, then referral to hospital is essential.

2 Health promotion. Dangers of smoking, emphasize the positive effect on giving up on the prognosis; also mention exercise and diet. Alcohol intake should be moderate.

3 Family history. Use in a positive way so that Stephen will follow advice. However, point out that techniques and methods of prevention have progressed considerably since his father had the condition.

4 Social circumstances. What support has he at home? Does he have a wife? What help can he obtain from his friends and peers?

5 Stress management. His occupation is associated with stress and he may be concerned about the question of redundancy. He may have been having problems with pupils and the support of his colleagues and headmaster is imperative. Would a short holiday be of benefit to him?

6 Hospital involvement. This could be required for diagnosis and treatment. If his angina is unstable, then he probably requires coronary angiogram with decisions made from this.

7 Patient's beliefs and expectations. With his definitive symptoms and his family history. What is concerning him and what does he feel the likely outcome will be?

4.3

Your next patient is Katy Jones, who is a 30-year-old secretary. She lives with her 34-year-old partner, who is a computer operator. She noticed a breast lump last night and is extremely worried. How would you manage this situation?

CONSTRUCTS

1 Patient's beliefs and expectations. Importance of patient autonomy. Does she think that she has cancer? Does she have any other thoughts to the aetiology or does she know about the condition? It is important to show her empathy and to care. Dealing with anger may be necessary.

2 Management options. Check signs and if you feel lump refer, in this age-group. Give feedback to patient according to your clinical suspicions.

3 Self-help gorups. This could be helpful if she is very worried, to talk to women who have been through a similar process.

4 Social circumstances. It is important to find out what support can be obtained from her family, colleagues and peers and also whether her partner will be supportive in this difficult situation.

5 Prognosis. You must be positive until a definite diagnosis is made but be realistic, depending on the findings.

6 Sexual health issues. Reassure her that, even in the worst scenario, with successful treatment she will continue a normal life and have a relationship with her partner which is unaltered.

7 Diagnostic possibilities. This will depend on the clinical findings but could be fibroma, fibrous tissue or carcinoma, and the doctor will have genuine management concerns in a situation like this.

4.4

Your next patient is Donald Murphy, a 68-year-old who has recently been attending the urology clinic. He lives with his 70-year-old wife, who is crippled with arthritis. He tells you that prostatic cancer has been diagnosed and that a letter is being sent to you. Discuss the issues which require discussion at this consultation.

CONSTRUCTS

1 Social circumstances. What help does his wife require? Is the house adapted to their needs? What family support do they have and what support from neighbours and community?

2 Understanding of problem. How are the symptoms affecting Donald? Discuss treatment with him with likely outcomes. Discuss how symptoms are likely to develop with the various treatment regimes.

3 Management options. This has a role both for the general practitioner and the practice team but also for the hospital in terms of treatment and if operation is necessary. With his situation at home it seems important that management should be carried out within the family context.

4 Follow-up. This should be both by the general practitioner and the hospital, with each knowing their respective roles.

5 Communication issues. This situation require empathy and a caring attitude. Be prepared to deal with anger and upset, as a lot is happening to the family in a short time span.

6 Care in the community. The family are in an ideal situation for support through this mechanism. Involve the caring agencies as required.

4.5

Your next patient is a 72-year-old, Michael Watt, whose wife died 4 weeks previously. He lives alone, although a daughter lives nearby. He has symptoms which are suggestive of depression. What are the important issues to be discussed at this consultation?

CONSTRUCTS

1 Patient understanding. Does he notice any difference in his own symptoms, in his sleeping and his eating? Does he have insight into what is happening? Important to involve him in decision-making. Does he understand the bereavement reaction?

2 Diagnosis of symptoms. Will require full history and examination to make proper diagnosis.

3 Social circumstances. What is the state of his house? Does he have any outside interests? What support does he have from his extended family, neighbours and community?

4 Patient outlook. Must understand the natural history of the bereavement reaction and should have other interests and support to help him through this.

5 Management issues. Caring with support from the practice team if necessary, with therapy being used if required. The risk of suicide must be assessed and this is a dilemma for the doctor, as there is considerable uncertainty about the outcome.

4.6

Your next patient is Maria Quigley, a 43-year-old housewife, who is distraught, having learned that her husband is having an affair. She consults about once annually and has no past history of note. She has two children, both of whom are away from home studying at university. How would you handle this consultation?

CONSTRUCTS

1 Family dynamics. Has she had any recent or medium-term problems with her marriage? Is she surprised at what has happened? Does she have support from their children, from her parents and her family?

2 Social circumstances. Does she have contact and support from her neighbours, from the church and from the community?

3 Other interests. Does she have work, either part-time or full-time?

4 Immediate care. Help in coming to terms with the situation. Be empathic and caring. The question of short-term sedation must be considered and help from Relate (marriage guidance).

5 Long-term care. More defined help from marriage guidance, the practice team and the social work department.

6 Communication issues. Use a style which deals with anger and is non-judgemental. Ask open questions. Use clarification and listening.

7 Patient's beliefs and expectations. From the present situation what would she like for the future and what would the husband like? Are these expectations realistic and something which both partners would agree to?

4.7

Irene Campbell, a 45-year-old, whom you have not seen for some time, requests HRT. She is an accountant and is unmarried. What issues arise and how would you handle this consultation?

CONSTRUCTS

1 Knowledge of HRT. What does she know about it? How accurate is her information? Is she aware of the benefits but also the side-effects and problems?

2 Reason for request. How bad are her symptoms? Is she having problems coming to terms with her age? Is there peer pressure regarding HRT? Does she have problems at work? What type of personality does she have and is there a hidden agenda?

3 Social factors. Is HRT accepted as being the norm for a business executive? Does she have pressure at work? Are there other interests outside her work? Do men play any part in her life and are they therefore a factor in the request?

4 Patient autonomy. What does she want? Is this based on a balanced view of the situation, weighing up the various factors?

5 Communication issues. Requires understanding and tact. Important to discuss with her without being judgemental.

6 Reaching decision. Is there evidence of a logical approach to decision-making?

4.8

Jason Campbell is a 24-year-old van-driver. He has been married for 5 years and has three children. He has been having recurrent dyspepsia for the last month. He admits to some difficulties making ends meet. What issues do you wish to cover at the consultation?

CONSTRUCTS

1 Family dynamics. How are things at home? Are there specific family pressures with three young children? Is there a lack of space and money?

2 Social issues. Is housing a problem? His work takes him away from home; does this add to the pressures on his wife? What support does she have from family, neighbourhood and community? Does he smoke and is there an excessive alcohol ingestion?

3 Health promotion. Give education regarding excercise, eating and symptoms, but also ask and give advice regarding smoking and drinking. Check BP as a preventive measure.

4 Cause of symptoms. Could be related to anxiety, excess alcohol intake, dietary.

5 Management. Once there is a definitive diagnosis, it is important to prevent and any cause should be removed and specific therapy given for symptoms. Support from the practice team would be a useful addition.

6 Patient's understanding. Does he know what is happening? What is his involvement in management and also the involvement of his family and the effect of his workplace? Is he willing to take preventive measures and therapy for symptoms when necessary?

4.9

Jim and Jean Blair are in their late 30s, both lawyers. They have decided that they would like to start a family and have made the appointment to discuss the genetic risks attached to this. How would you handle this consultation?

CONSTRUCTS

1 Patients' knowledge. Middle-class and as lawyers likely to have knowledge of situation where matters can go wrong. Assess their level of knowledge and who has advised them on this.

2 Family dynamics. Does their marriage seem OK? Do they have family support? Are they both happy at work?

3 Ethical issues. An abnormality could be found when any screening is carried out and it is difficult to predict the consequences. If a major defect, would they consider an abortion?

4 Couple's psyche. Are they robust, in a stable relationship and could they cope with difficulties which arose?

5 Communication issues. As this is a delicate area, must be handled with sensitivity. Opportunity for involvement of the practice team.

6 Sexual health issues. If a problem arises, this could affect their relationship.

7 Risk assessment. They must realize both the up side and the down side and with understanding agree a plan with the doctor.

4.10

Mary Fegan is aged 43 and a frequent attender at the surgery. She has long abused alcohol and suffers from short-term memory loss and poor decision-making. She has been unemployed for 3 years and has changed house three times in the past year. She calls asking for a tranquillizer as life events are getting on top of her. How would you handle this consultation?

CONSTRUCTS

1 Health education. Important to outline effects of long-term tranquillizers and how these can be related to other issues.

2 Patient autonomy. It is important that she is part of the decision-making. Does she accept that she has a role in this? What does Mary see as the way forward?

3 Social circumstances. Does she have problem with housing? Does she smoke? What are her other interests and does she have help from neighbours and others in the community?

4 Treatment options. This involves the practice team and could entail counselling. The question of medication should also be considered.

5 Patient's understanding. Does she understand the processes? The ownership of the problem is important, with her involvement in this and in any therapy.

Commentary 4

This surgery has a breadth which deals with the physical, social and psychological aspects of general practice, with prevention, genetic counselling, social problems which have a physical overlay of alcohol, bereavement and a potential marital breakup. Constructs included are health promotion, patient understanding, stress management, the role of the hospital, sexual health issues, doctor's dilemma and patient request.

MEQ 5

5.1

It is Monday morning and your first patient is John, aged 54. He is fat and a smoker and has known IHD, as do his two brothers. He comes to ask you if it is worth his while applying for a Large Goods Vehicle (LGV) licence. Outline your response.

CONSTRUCTS

1 Communication skills. How aware is the candidate of the need to clearly discuss this?

2 Patient's point of view. Recognition of the need to know patient's reasons.

3 Medicolegal factors. Understanding of the legal implications of LGV certification.

4 Social factors. Recognition of financial or employment pressures.

5 Health education. Is an opportunity taken to discuss preventive care?

6 Management issues. Set action plan with patient.

5.2

At the end of the consultation, while he is there, John wonders if you can help him with his toe. Removing his shoe and sock you find that his left great toe is swollen and purulent and has a nail that is cut back 'hard'. What is your diagnosis and how would you manage this consultation?

CONSTRUCTS

1 **Diagnostic skills.** Do they make the correct diagnosis?

2 **Communication skills.** Do they use suitable language?

3 **Health education.** Do they outline preventive measures?

4 **Management.** Is the management correct?

5 **Teamwork.** Do they consider involving other team members?

5.3

Your next patient is Fiona. She is 60 and complains of cystitis. She has burning, dysuria and frequency. Outline your consultation.

CONSTRUCTS

1 **Clinical skills.** A skilful consultation and suitable examination?

2 **Preventive skills.** Recognition of factors such as the menopause.

3 **Psychosexual skills.** Recognition that there may be a sexual dimension.

4 **Follow-up arrangements.** Adequate follow-up arranged.

5.4

Thomas, who is 50, has had recurrent indigestion for most of the time that you have known him. In 1972 he had a barium meal, which showed he had a DU. He wants the new tablets his friend has got. What would you wish to cover in the consultation?

CONSTRUCTS

1 **Consultation skills.** An adequate consultation?

2 Recognition of patient's point of view. Are patient's views explored?

3 Cost-effective investigation. Is planned management cost-effective?

4 Eradication therapy. Is *Helicobacter pylori* considered?

5 Caritas. Does the candidate care?

5.5

Jim attends for his routine prescription review. He has had asthma for some years. He works as a binman and is quite happy with the way things are going. Reviewing his prescription you note that he uses lots of salbutamol inhalers but rarely orders his steroid inhaler. Proceed.

CONSTRUCTS

1 Clinical skills. Recognizes the need for prophylaxis?

2 Consultation skills. Carries out an effective consultation?

3 Patient's point of view. Why the patient acts as he does.

4 Social factors. Social class as a factor in his management.

5 Follow-up skills. Recognizes this need.

6 Preventive skills. Shows evidence of the need for health promotion.

7 Involvement of other team members. Considers using other team members' skills.

5.6

A very frightened Ann comes in next. She is 18 and after blushing tells you she has a sore ear. Examination reveals no abnormality. What thoughts go through your mind?

CONSTRUCTS

1 Awareness of patient's hidden agenda. Does the patient have another reason for attending?

2 Consultation skills. Skills to discover that reason?

3 Patient expectations. What does patient hope to get from the consultation?

5.7

She smiles at you after your explanation and tells you that she would like to go on the pill. She is social class 5, gets an occasional migraine attack and has been sexually active since she was 16.

CONSTRUCTS

1 Clinical skills. Recognizes the consultation problems and considers other therapeutic options.

2 Consultation skills. A caring consultation?

3 Recognition of patient's point of view. Non-judgemental.

4 Social influences. Knowledge of locality.

5 Follow-up arrangements. Recognizes need.

5.8

Jimmy is a rare attender. He comes in and asks for a sick note because he has to stay at home for a couple of weeks to look after his elderly mother. How do you respond?

CONSTRUCTS

1 Consultation skills. A suitable consultation?

2 Doctor's point of view. Recognizes doctor's role and feeling about request.

3 Patient's point of view. Understands patient's reasons for request.

4 Ethical considerations. Understands the law re certification.

5 Caritas. Candidate cares.

6 Use of team. Considers use of other members of team, e.g. social worker.

5.9

Margaret is depressed. She has been seeing you for some weeks. Her marriage is breaking down and she is the 'guilty party'. She is not improving. She asks, 'What should I do, doctor?' Outline your response.

CONSTRUCTS

1 Consultation skills. Recognition of options rather than solutions.

2 Recognition of patient's point of view. Recognizes need for them to talk.

3 Awareness of doctor's own feeling. Recognition of need not to be judgemental.

4 Use of team. Uses skills of other team members, e.g. CPN.

5 Caritas. Candidate cares.

5.10

Your surgery is interrupted by Betty Bloggs, a social worker, who has rung up and would like you to tell her about Susan Jones, one of your patients, who has ME. Proceed.

CONSTRUCTS

1 Ethical constraints. Recognition of need to confirm credentials and try and protect confidentiality.

2 Consultations skills. A caring consultation that does not upset the social worker.

3 Caritas. Recognizes the need to balance patient's needs against ethical considerations.

4 Expectations of social worker. What does she wish from contact?

Commentary 5

Deals with two common surgery situations of patients who present with something when they are really concerned about another matter. It also contains the common situation of patients asking for tablets which their friends have and which they have probably taken before their consultation. It also deals with two difficult ethical issues of the patient asking for a sick note and the phone call from the social worker. The constructs which are more prevalent in this surgery are diagnostic skills, teamwork, psychosexual issues, cost-effective investigation, caritas, hidden agenda and ethical constraints.

MEQ 6

6.1

Damian is a drug addict and is known to be violent. He attends without an appointment. How do you manage this situation?

CONSTRUCTS

1 Consultation skills. Recognizes special skills required.

2 Teamwork. Recognizes the problems addicts cause to reception staff.

3 Doctor's own feelings. Shows evidence of not being judgemental.

4 Social factors. Recognizes the problems of drug addicition.

6.2

Damian wants 'a few temazepam' and seems to be under the influence of drugs. How do you proceed?

CONSTRUCTS

1 Clinical skills. Does the candidate have a logical plan?

2 Consultation skills. Does the candidate complete this consultation without inducing a violent response?

3 Follow-up plans. Does the candidate consider the long-term care of this patient?

4 Teamwork. Does the candidate consider other agencies, e.g. CPN or drug unit?

6.3

Your next patient is Beverley, a sweet little girl of 3 who makes her mother's life a misery by never sleeping at night. How do you manage this consultation?

CONSTRUCTS

1 Consultation skills. Is the consultation carried out in a caring manner?

2 Management skills. Does the candidate recognize the variety of options available?

3 Teamwork. Does the candidate involve other members of the team?

4 Follow-up. Is there clear evidence of follow-up?

6.4

Alice rings you during surgery. She is pregnant for the second time and it is 14 weeks since her last period. She tells you that she has had a show of blood. How would you proceed?

CONSTRUCTS

1 Consultation skills. Is this a caring and appropriate consultation?

2 Patient's views of problem. Does the candidate elicit these?

3 Caritas. Does the candidate understand the anxiety in this situation?

4 Follow-up. Are appropriate follow-up arrangements made?

6.5

Mrs Lacey brings Natalie, who is 3. She wonders if she is getting migraine like her dad. She is hot and full of cold and complaining of a headache. Outline how you would proceed.

CONSTRUCTS

1 Consultation skills. Is this an appropriate consultation?

2 Examination skills. Are appropriate measures carried out?

3 Patient's views. Does the candidate elicit the mother's views of headache and migraine?

4 Health education. Is this consultation used to educate?

6.6

Your practice manager pops in to tell you that a patient wishes to complain about the practice assistant's management of his son. How would you deal with this situation?

CONSTRUCTS

1 Practice dynamics. Understanding the importance of solving this problem.

2 The assistant's views. Does the candidate discover the assistant's view of the situation?

3 The patient's views. Does the candidate discover the patient's view of what has happened?

4 Medicolegal aspects. Does the candidate understand that there may be service committee or litigation implications of this situation?

5 Use of the team. Does the candidate involve the manager in the exercise?

6 Follow-up. Is the complaint followed up and conciliation attempted if this is appropriate?

6.7

Your investigation revealed, thankfully, that there had merely been a misunderstanding between the patient and the doctor and the problem is solved with informal discussion. You note, however, when reviewing the doctor's record of the case that he has been giving an 8-year-old child soluble aspirin. What are the implications of this?

CONSTRUCTS

1 Clinical knowledge. Does the candidate understand the danger of aspirin in young children?

2 Implications for practice population. Has this been widely prescribed for young children by this doctor?

3 Audit. Can the population be identified and their records reviewed?

4 Education. How does the candidate plan to educate the involved doctor?

5 Medicolegal aspects. Does the candidate understand the medicolegal implications of this prescription?

6.8

Your next patient is Donald. He is a new patient who tells you he is having treatment for his prostate from his previous doctor. Reviewing his notes, you find that he is receiving pharmacological treatment for prostatism without having had any baseline investigation of his blood or urological examinations. What are the implications for you in this consultation?

CONSTRUCTS

1 Clinical diagnosis. Does the candidate recognize the need for a clear diagnosis?

2 Communication skills. Is the candidate able to tactfully arrange for correct investigation?

3 Medicolegal aspects. Might there be legal consequences for the previous doctor?

4 Management issues. Agrees action plan with patient.

6.9

The next patient is Susan Jones, your patient with ME. She is very angry because no one takes her seriously and she feels so unwell. Proceed.

CONSTRUCTS

1 Consultation skills. How does the candidate manage the consultation?

2 Patient's point of view. Recognizes the patient has true symptoms.

3 Doctor's feelings. Recognizes doctor impotence.

4 Follow-up arrangements. Recognizes need.

6.10

She is seeing a doctor in a town some miles away for gamma globulin injections. She asks you if she should continue seeing him. How do you respond?

CONSTRUCTS

1 Consultation skills. Carries out a helpful consultation.

2 Ethical factors. How do the patient and doctor view the other doctor's therapy?

3 Patient's point of view. Recognizes a patient's right to choose.

4 Long-term relationship. Recognizes the importance of a long-term relationship with a patient like this.

5 Caritas. Shows he/she cares.

Commentary 6

This surgery deals with some common symptoms in general practice: headache, anxious mother and also the problem of complaints. The surgery has the problem of a patient attending another practitioner and also the problem of inappropriate prescribing by a partner. The constructs in this surgery which have had limited mention before are clinical skills, social factors, practice dynamics, audit, education and long-term relationship.

MEQ 7

Your first patient, Michael Stuart, age 16, presents with a sore throat. He says his mother has sent him to get an antibiotic because he has some important examinations coming up. Describe with reasons your response and your management of Michael.

CONSTRUCTS

1 Clinical activity. The history (questions asked) and examination and the way these contribute to an assessment of the patient.

2 Clinical understanding. Epidemiology of sore throats; evidence for value of antibiotics. The rationale for the ideal management in terms of the epidemiology of sore throats (the high likelihood of viral infections and the self-limiting nature of the majority, even of bacterial infections). The expected effect of antibiotics on the clinical course of the disease.

3 Understanding of family as a system. Show an understanding of the role of the mother and the likely effect on the health beliefs of both mother and Michael. Explore the relationship of a 16-year-old youth with his mother, including areas of possible conflict.

4 Respect for the ideas, concerns and expectations of the patient and his family. Show how the ideas, concerns and expectations of the patient affected the nature of the reply. A positive response to the patient's request not necessarily required, but in the event of a refusal of antibiotics would show that the patient's views were being respected, and his needs being taken into account. Show respect for the (absent) mother.

5 The ability to negotiate a treatment plan. Show evidence of negotiation. Avoid both blunt refusal (even with explanation) and passive acceptance. Show concern to give continuing care – e.g. how to contact help if situation changes.

7.2

The next patient is a postgraduate student from Iran, age 23, who has just registered with the practice. He has been troubled by frequent, loose motions five to six times a day for the last 3 weeks. He has not had similar symptoms before. He feels unwell and admits he is finding his new course very stressful. How would you manage this consultation?

CONSTRUCTS

1 Rational clinical approach. Show a rational approach to elucidation of this symptom in terms of the questions asked and the examination and investigations performed. These would be relevant to the background of the patient. Concentrate on a general practice approach, showing some evidence of hypotheticodeductive thinking and avoiding the initial use of expensive secondary-care investigations. The wording stresses *this* consultation and marks would not be given for detailed descriptions of investigations that might be required at a later stage.

2 Appropriate range of diagnostic possibilities. Show a range of possibilities exist, from a simple infection or stress-related bowel disorder to inflammatory bowel disease. Discuss the likelihood of different possibilities and the importance of recognition of more serious conditions (such as inflammatory bowel disease). Show how factors such as recent overseas residence affect the probabilities. Avoid prolonged discussion of conditions, such as neoplasms, that would be rare, bearing in mind factors such as the age of the patient.

3 The ideas, concerns and expectations of the patient. Show the influence of the ideas and expectations of the patient and how these may be affected by background culture and the health care system in his home country. Explore the effect of the current social situation (a newly arrived postgraduate starting on a long educational course) on the expectations. Discuss how the stressfulness of the course is explored. Identify other current possible causes of stress (loneliness, finance, uncertainty).

4 Approaches to communication. Show the need to use a range of communication skills, such as open exploration, clarification and listening. Show how the patient's stress and uncertainty can be relieved by explanation both of the possibilities and of the management plan and the way that plan will be implemented in our health system.

7.3

Your next patient should have been Pam David, age 50. She attended the previous evening with a lump in her neck and you found marked lymphadenopathy. You invited her back for further tests. She fails to attend. How would you respond to this situation?

CONSTRUCTS

1 Patient orientation. Show an understanding of the reasons a patient might avoid further investigation of a threatening symptom. Describe a range of feelings the patient might be experiencing. Show the need for the doctor to understand and accept such feelings.

2 Doctor's feelings. Explore the possible anxieties of the doctor. Discuss the doctor's feelings about the previous consultation and any relationship between that and current non-attendance – including failure to explain or to deal with patient fear.

3 Medical responsibility. Show a sense of responsibility for the welfare of a patient, even when that patient fails to attend. Discuss how this can conflict with respect for patient autonomy. Discuss areas in which the priority will be for some form of intervention. Discuss medicolegal issues, such as documentation.

4 Intervention strategies. Present a range of possible intervention strategies (visiting; telephone calls in person or through reception staff; personal letter or further appointments). Discuss the pros and cons of each. Show which intervention strategy is preferred and give reasons for this.

7.4

John Peter is a 40-year-old self-employed decorator. He attends with a 3-day history of back pain. He says he has been resting but the pain has not improved. He asks if you could recommend a good chiropractor. How would you respond?

CONSTRUCTS

1 Appropriate assessment of back pain. Discuss the history and examination that should be carried out. Detail aetiological factors. Detail effects on patient. Detail findings that would cause concern about nerve root pressure. Detail prognostic factors (these would include psychological and occupational factors).

2 Appropriate management of back pain. Discuss the place of limited rest and exercise. Discuss the analgesia required, and how best provided. Discuss the role of physical treatments and manipulation. Discuss time off work. Refer to modern guidelines being produced on back pain. Discuss evidence and reasons for changes in proposed management in recent years.

3 Relationship with alternative practitioners. Discuss the range of practitioners who might be involved (including osteopath/physiotherapist). Discuss the role of a chiropractor, and the procedures they use. Discuss evidence for the effectiveness of chiropractor. Discuss the registration of alternative practitioners. Show an honest appreciation of the mixture of feelings that can affect the relationship between medical and alternative practitioners.

4 Appraisal of effectiveness. Consider patient's expectations (re effective care). Discuss the difficulties in assessing the effectiveness of procedures. Discuss 'good' in terms of outcome and process (i.e. caring approach, etc.). Realize that such appraisal is also difficult in terms of specialist colleagues.

5 Patient choice in the referral process. Explore the difficulties in negotiation when a patient makes a specific request. Discuss the information that would need to be provided for the patient. Discuss alternative sources of information (e.g. recommendations by friends). Explore the process whereby patients are enabled to make an informed choice.

7.5

Anne Cane is aged 28 and the mother of four children. Her husband had a vasectomy 3 years ago. She presented with a 3-month history of amenorrhoea, but insisted that she had not had any other partners. A pregnancy test has now been reported as positive. Describe your approach.

CONSTRUCTS

1 Appropriate range of explanations. Explore the likelihood of a failure of the vasectomy, giving reasons and relating to operative method. Explore the possibility that the patient may not be telling the truth about other sexual contacts, either their existence or their extent.

2 Making contact with the patient. Show sensitive handling of the initial provision of information. Anticipate patient reactions, including denial, anger or an acute depressive reaction. Describe methods of dealing with these that would maintain contact. Be non-judgemental.

3 Management within the family context. Show that this event is likely to affect the whole family. Discuss the reactions that might be expected in the family. Discuss the possibility of and the patient's attitude to bringing the husband into the decisions. Discuss approaches to confirm whether the vasectomy has failed.

4 Provision of a range of options. Explore the legal aspects of termination. Explore the advantages and disadvantages of termination. Explore the support required for a continuation of the pregnancy, such as counsellors. Show a respect for patient choice of option. Enable patient to consider her options over time (including follow-up appointment).

7.6

Ellen Tudor brings in her 6-year-old child, Sophie. Sophie has been diagnosed as having 'glue ear'. The mother says that the local hospital has told her the child should be admitted for insertion of grommets, but there is a 6-month waiting-list. She ask your advice as to whether she should go privately. Discuss the factors you would consider in your reply.

CONSTRUCTS

1 Assessment of effectiveness of procedures. Show knowledge of evidence about the effectiveness (or otherwise) of grommets in the management of 'glue ear'. Discuss the application of this evidence to the patient in question. Discuss alternative approaches.

2 Assessment of needs of the individual. Show an understanding of how assessment of individual patients can lead to deviation from evidence-based approaches. Show how the information received from the hospital (or community audiology) can allow discussion of the risks and prognosis for this individual. Discuss the parents' views of the effects of the 'glue ear' and the needs of the individual.

3 The structure of health care provision. Explore the role of general practitioners in setting and working with contracts for secondary care. Explore the current status of private health care provision. Explore the range of attitudes to such private provision. Show a need to evaluate the patient's attitudes to such provision.

4 Cost–benefit assessment. Consider how the costs of private treatment might be met, and the personal effect of these on the individuals concerned. Consider the likely economic effects on the family in the light of anticipated benefits in management.

7.7

You took a smear from Diana Platt, a student of 19. This has been reported as being unsatisfactory and showing Trichomonas. Diana's mother telephones to say that Diana has now gone to France for a year and has asked her to ring for the result of the smear. How would you manage this conversation?

CONSTRUCTS

1 Confidentiality (ethical dilemma). The importance of confidentiality. The factors that would allow such issues to be overridden (ranging from prior permission to degree of seriousness of the situation). Issues relating to informing (and treating) any patient through a third party, especially in the absence of being able to explain, negotiate and instruct.

2 Assessment of risk. An understanding of the levels of risk in this situation, both to the patient and to any partners. An assessment of the urgency with which action should be taken.

3 Communication. Discuss the advantages and disadvantages of a range of options that might be used to overcome the problems of confidentiality: refusing to divulge; taking no action until patient herself makes contact; requesting a forwarding address; providing limited information to the mother that the test was unsatisfactory and needs to be repeated.

7.8

A visit is made to a man of 74 with angina. He tells you his wife is due to be discharged from hospital following a stroke. Apparently she still has considerable difficulty in walking and finds it hard to get the right words on occasion. He is very worried about his ability to cope. Discuss how you would plan the continuing care of this couple.

CONSTRUCTS

1 Understanding of principles of care in the community. Give a brief description of the Community Care Act. Explain the role of social services departments. Discuss how contact can be made with the appropriate personnel (care managers).

2 Elicitation of patient wishes. Show an appreciation of the need to explore the underlying wishes of both patients. Show why immediately expressed concerns may not be the true wishes. Explore the difficulties in communication that might occur because of the CVA suffered by the wife.

3 Understanding the working of the PHCT. Explore the roles of a range of PHCT members, including community nurses, physiotherapists and speech therapists. Discuss how these may be co-ordinated. Discuss the concept of 'key workers' and make proposals for appropriate key worker.

4 Physical and psychological care of the husband. Give equal consideration to the needs of the husband. Show how his angina might be assessed and treated. Show how his fears can be allayed. Provide a system (including an 'emergency call procedure') for crisis management.

5 Liaison with hospital. Consider role of hospital in long-term follow-up. Consider the role of hospital liaison/link workers with community. Consider possibilities for respite care.

7.9

One partner suggests that there is an increased amount of violence in the practice area and they are no longer happy about doing evening or weekend visits to certain parts of the practice unaccompanied. Discuss the issues facing the practice.

CONSTRUCTS

1 Objective assessment. Consider whether the increased amount of violence is real. Consider the opinions of other workers, including nurses and police. Consider how widespread the problem is and whether limited to a few patients or areas.

2 Continuity of care. Discuss the concept of 24-hour cover and its relation to continuity of care. Provide a realistic assessment of the existence of such continuity in the current health service. Discuss a range of patients (e.g. terminal care) where such continuity might be considered a priority.

3 Alternative out-of-hours provision. Discuss the range of out-of-hours facilities available today, including co-operatives, deputizing and emergency centres. Discuss the advantages and disadvantages of these. Specifically discuss how they can cope better in situations of increased violence.

4 Cost–benefit. Discuss the financial implications of a decision. Discuss how to measure the relative importance of financial, emotional and security factors.

5 Partnership decision-making. Consider factors (such as gender, age, health and attitude) that might affect personal decisions on such matters. Consider the risks of conflict in issues such as this. Discuss strategies to avoid conflict.

7.10

A brainstorm of the practice staff was carried out to decide on the next round of practice audit activity. The following list was produced. Choose three items and give brief arguments for their inclusion.

- Alcohol problems.
- Accessibility of the surgery to the disabled.
- Acne.
- Benign prostatic hyperplasia.
- Influenza vaccination.
- Repeat prescription procedures.
- The red eye.
- Vaginal discharge.

CONSTRUCTS

For each chosen area the following constructs should be considered.

1 Relevance. Show how the chosen subject is important for the practice and the service it provides. This might be because of risk, prevalence or social concern. Show evidence of benefits from achieving an audit target.

2 Feasibility. Show how the chosen subject could effectively be audited. Show how information could be collected. Show how standards might be obtained or set. Show how changes could be proposed and implemented.

3 Personal and professional growth. Show evidence of personal commitment to or enjoyment of the subject. Explain how it might lead to an area of personal development or obtaining a professional skill.

4 Team building. Show how the different members of the PHCT might be involved. Show how this could develop the team as a functioning unit.

Commentary 7

Deals with important problems, some of which are the 'bread-and-butter' of general practice, e.g. sore throat and loose motions, and also brings into play some of the other factors which affect everyday work, e.g. patients not returning, the availability of private medicine, the increasing problems of violence affecting doctors and also quality assurance with responsibility for standards of work. The constructs used in this include ability to negotiate treatment, patient orientation, doctor's feelings, medical responsibility, relationship with alternate practitioner, choice and referral process, assessment of need, structure of health care provision, alternative out-of-hours, partnership decision-making, personal and professional growth and team building.

MEQ 8

8.1

Your first patient, Stephen Owen, a medical student of 24, presents with a painful rash on the left buttock. It has been present for 3 days. You diagnose herpes zoster. He tells you that he had thought this was possible and asks whether antiviral creams or tablets would help him. Discuss your response.

CONSTRUCTS

1 Understanding of the way management should be based on evidence. Show awareness of the value of antivirals in the treatment of herpetic infections. Show awareness of evidence for the appropriate mode of administration. Show awareness of evidence about time of beginning treatment. (Details of the evidence would not be required.)

2 Coping with physical symptoms and distress. Show an appreciation of the importance of ensuring adequate physical relief. Detail a rational approach to pain relief, including both range of analgesic and administration. Show awareness of the side-effects of commonly used medications and how to cope with these.

3 Exploration of patient beliefs. Exhibit awareness that the background of the patient (a medical student) and the nature of the question asked do not necessarily imply a good understanding of the problem. Show how patient beliefs might be explored. Discuss possible patient concerns, such as effects on current activity, work situation and potential exams, and effects on people who might be in contact with him.

8.2

Your next patient, Peter Abel, requests PCC for his girlfriend. He says that a condom failed the previous night, but she is too embarrassed to attend herself. Discuss, with reasons, how you would respond.

CONSTRUCTS

1 Ethical issues. Show an appreciation of a range of ethical dilemmas posed by this consultation, including: issues relating to confidentiality and how much the girlfriend's treatment can be discussed *in absentia*; issues relating to treating any patient through a third party, especially in the absence of being able to explain, negotiate and instruct; issues relating to the specific understanding of the moral nature of PCC (possibly acting post-fertilization) and obtaining informed consent for its use.

2 Patient orientation. An understanding of the personal embarrassment that may be felt. A concern to discover a positive response to the need. An awareness of the risks of failing to respond to the request.

3 Communication. Discuss a range of options that might be used to negotiate with the boyfriend, including an exploration of specific barriers that might increase embarrassment and ways of overcoming these. Specific evidence of attempts to make contact, to clarify the situation, to negotiate and to provide safety nets.

8.3

The next patient is Lachmi Singh, a 62-year-old woman with DM. She comes with her daughter, who requests a repeat prescription of glibenclamide and paracetamol. You note that Mrs Singh has not had blood (including HbA_1C) checked for 15 months. She did not respond to an invitation to attend the practice diabetic miniclinic. How might you manage this situation?

CONSTRUCTS

1 Clinical knowledge. Show a rational approach to the management of maturity-onset diabetes, which includes: an understanding of how to assess control of the condition; an understanding of the importance of early diagnosis of complications; discussion of the priority to be attached to the various examinations and tests.

2 Patient orientation. Show understanding of reasons patients fail to respond to management protocols for chronic illness. Explore factors such as: language and cultural barriers; failure of understanding of the nature of the condition; patient health beliefs; personal priorities and pressures on patients.

3 Communication. How doctors might explore the reasons for patients' reluctance. The importance of sensitive and non-judgemental approaches. The use of interpretation. The problems of communicating through a family member.

4 Teamwork in general practice. Show how the doctor might involve other team members in the management. Possible roles for practice nurses and optometrists (and also dietitians and chiropodists). The use of link workers. Show how the involvement of team members might be negotiated.

8.4

Your next patient is Roger Dane, age 56. He has been to see a gastroenterologist because of persistent abdominal discomfort. He brings a handwritten note from the consultant asking you to prescribe a new drug and giving the name of the supplier. You have not heard of this drug and there is no information in the *BNF*. What dilemmas does this request confront you with and how might they be resolved?

CONSTRUCTS

1 Prescribing responsibility. The legal responsibility for prescribing. The legal risks of prescribing an unlicensed preparation. The availability of information to discharge this responsibility.

2 Relationships with hospital. Respective responsibilities of general practitioner and consultant. The need for effective and detailed communication. The pressures on general practitioners to maintain good relationships with their colleagues.

3 Financial constraints. The pressures on hospital budgets. The pressures on general practitioners' budgets, including incentive schemes under indicative prescribing budgets and fund-holding drug budgets.

4 The use of professional advice. List sources of professional advice, such as prescribing advisers of health authorities/commissions, defence organizations and pharmaceutical firms. Discuss how to make the best use of these resources.

8.5

During the surgery the receptionist asks you to speak to Dermot Stephens, who is requesting an urgent call on the telephone. This 70-year-old man suffers from acute panic attacks, but also has known COAD and IHD. He has already had three emergency calls this week because he says he is breathless. Discuss the options available to you in the management of this man.

CONSTRUCTS

1 The general practitioner's role. The need for reassessment of the physical and mental state of the patient. The decision as to whether to seek to modify patient behaviour or to accept and contain the frequent calls. The decision as to whether to seek to make a contract with the patient. The decision as to whether to refer for further help.

2 The role of the primary health care team. What instructions it would be acceptable to leave with or convey through reception staff. The use that might be made of nursing staff to make initial assessments. The skills that might be available within the primary care team to manage anxiety states.

3 The role of secondary care. Secondary care resources (including psychiatry, psychology and CPNs) that might have a part to play in the management of this situation.

4 Time. The issue of time management in the middle of a surgery. The effects of recurrent demands on the nature of the decisions that might be taken. An honest appraisal of the feelings of those involved.

8.6

After surgery the practice manager says that there has been trouble at reception because a patient was demanding an appointment that day and all the appointments were full. Discuss the roles of different members of the PHCT in producing an answer to this problem.

CONSTRUCTS

1 Factors in appointment system problem. Show an appreciation of reasons why difficulties in appointment systems can arise. Explore a range of factors, including increased demand (short- and long-term), decreased provision (short-term, such as illness, and long-term), lack of flexibility, general practice activity (booking surgeries well in advance), etc. Discuss how the underlying problem in this instance could be assessed.

2 Understanding of team roles. Discuss the roles of each member of the PHCT. Show the key role of management skills (e.g. practice manager) in assessing and resolving such problems. Discuss the ability of nurses to assess urgency. Discuss the role of reception staff in administering an effective system. Show that medical roles include responsibility for ensuring accessibility.

3 Flexibility. Propose a range of solutions. Show the need for flexibility in staff roles. Consider the advantages and disadvantages of practice nurses seeing patients presenting acutely. Consider the advantages and disadvantages of having some degree of open access.

8.7

There is a request for a visit to Naomi Root, age 23. She is 9 weeks pregnant and bleeding vaginally. She lost a previous pregnancy at 12 weeks. Discuss your management of this situation.

CONSTRUCTS

1 Clinical assessment. The physical examination required to make an assessment, including the extent of bleeding (pulse, BP, etc.). The appropriate extent of gynaecological examination in this situation.

2 Psychosocial assessment. The patient's attitude to the previous miscarriage. The patient's attitude to the present pregnancy. The attitude of other key members in the patient's social support, including partner, parents and close friends. The patient's level of distress.

3 Management options. The range of management options, together with evidence for their value, including: inaction (wait and see); rest (including being off work) at home; admission for observation; indications for urgent admission.

4 Patient-orientated decision-making. Patient understanding of the situation and the management options. Patient expectations. The extent to which management for which there is little evidence should be instituted in response to patient concerns.

8.8

At the practice meeting it is intended to discuss the appointment of new staff. One partner is very keen to employ a counsellor. Another partner would like an extra practice nurse to develop chronic disease clinics. Discuss the factors that should be considered in the decision.

CONSTRUCTS

1 Evidence of value. Evidence that a counsellor in the practice can improve outcome for patients. Evidence that separate chronic disease clinics can improve outcome for patients. Evidence for practice nurse-run clinics being effective.

2 Practice needs. Current provision within the practice. How level of expected use of either innovation might be determined.

3 Cost. The costs to the practice. Resources that might be used to fund these developments, including FHSA policy in funding posts.

4 Personal commitment. The need to discover views of individual practice members. The importance of views of key workers in a field. The danger of overreaction to the views of certain members.

8.9

The practice manager tells you that during the year the cost of deputizing service use has risen by 50%. Discuss the implications of this statement.

CONSTRUCTS

1 Out-of-hours workload. Changes in out-of-hours workload and the reasons for this, including: change in expectations of patients; change in availability and accessibility of daytime services.

2 Attitudes to working antisocial hours. Changes in doctors' attitudes to working antisocial hours, including: different family and personal commitments; risks of violence; changed behaviour in hospital years.

3 Finance. The ways that the use of deputizing services is funded (directly and through practice expense reimbursement). Changes in the funding of out-of-hours work. Effects on other provisions of the practice.

4 Management of change. Need for ascertaining individual concerns and needs of doctors. Alternative approaches to improving service to patients, such as extended surgery hours or the use of emergency centres.

8.10

Below are listed the five key areas from the Health of the Nation strategy. Choose three and write brief targets for a practice policy to address them.
• Coronary heart disease and stroke.
• Cancers.
• Mental illness.
• HIV/AIDS.
• Accidents.

CONSTRUCTS

For each chosen area the following constructs should be considered.

1 Relevance. Show how the chosen subject is related to practice needs. State the benefits expected from achieving the targets.

2 Clinical value. Provide evidence that the chosen targets effectively alter outcomes.

3 Realizability. Provide targets that can be achieved: within a limited time; at reasonable cost in money and staff; in a way that is acceptable to patients.

Commentary 8

This surgery deals with practical situations of patients attending for new medication with a product not yet in the *BNF*, but also deals with the practice development of appointment systems, the presence of a counsellor in general practice and also the practice's response to the changing out-of-hours situation. In addition, it deals with common conditions, such as herpes zoster, and with PCC. The constructs included here are evidence-based patient orientation, clinical knowledge, prescribing response, financial constraints, use of professional advice, time, understanding team roles, patient-orientated decision-making, personal commitments, attitudes to working out-of-hours and management of change.

MEQ 9

9.1

Michelle Moore, a 13-year-old girl, attends your morning surgery. She tells you that she is concerned because her periods are infrequent (every 10 weeks) and painful. You notice in the records that she saw a partner in the practice with the same complaint 1 month ago and had a pregnancy test carried out, which was negative. What issues are raised by this consultation?

CONSTRUCTS

1 Normal physiology. Menstrual pattern described is not unusual and does not indicate disease. Discuss the normal menarche. Irregular infrequent periods common at this age. Less likely to be painful at this age but pain can be related to patient's perception.

2 Communication issues. Complaint may be a way in to request contraception. Point out that patients may present their problems indirectly. Doctor's approach will then determine if real problem is brought out. Particular case is a sensitive issue and patient may feel unsure of doctor's possible response.

3 Sexual health issues. Contraception and risk of pregnancy – is she having intercourse? What method of contraception is she using? Risk of STDs? Should you push to have a smear done? Note the previous pregnancy test. The need to explore this area and to find out if the girl is at risk of pregnancy or STDs. Possible prescribing of OCP and possible need for smear at some point.

4 Ethical issues. Can you prescribe contraception? Should you? Should parents be told? Should you raise contraception issue yourself? Dilemmas of offering contraceptive advice to young girls, including the question as to whether or not doctors are allowed to prescribe and whether or not parents should be involved. Issues of psychological maturity of the girl and her current sexual and contraceptive behaviour.

5 Practice issues. Should partner have done more? Follow-up? Policy on under-age contraception? Queries the handling of the previous consultation. States that partner should have attempted to explore sexual activity and contraceptive use. Suggests that partners should have a policy on under-age contraception. Mentions large number of unplanned pregnancies in teenagers.

9.2

During your coffee break you receive a phone call from Kate Campbell, a friend who is not a patient. She tells you she is about to go on holiday to Tanzania, and asks if you could supply her with some ciprofloxacin for use if she develops infective diarrhoea. How might you respond?

CONSTRUCTS

1 Prescribing for someone who is not a patient. Knows that you cannot issue an NHS prescription to someone who is not a patient but is aware that you could issue a private prescription. Is aware that this would be expensive. Mentions the ethical problems of treating someone else's patient.

2 Mixing work with friendship. Points out the hazards of providing medical care for friends. Discusses the desirability of separating medical practice from private life. Suggests ways in which the doctor could tactfully refer the women back to her own doctor.

3 Usefulness of antibiotics in this situation – practical therapeutics. Aware that the drug has been shown to be effective in traveller's diarrhoea, and aware of the costs and potential side-effects.

4 Other measures to be taken. Discusses other aspects of illness prevention – immunizations, malaria prophylaxis, food hygiene, ice in drinks, HIV.

9.3

Your next patient, Ian Ferguson, is a man aged 55 who normally works as a gardener. He has been off work for several weeks after a wrist fracture, which is still causing him some pain. It seems unlikely that he will be able to return to operating heavy machinery. He asks you if you would support his request for early retirement on health grounds. How would you respond?

CONSTRUCTS

1 Patient's ideas. What does the patient think? What the patient thinks about the idea of early retirement and how he sees his future. Explore the patient's feelings about being asked to consider this.

2 Patient's understanding. Does he understand the implications of taking early retirement? Ensure that the patient is aware that he is unlikely to receive long-term sickness benefit. If the patient is at any time thought to be fit to do 'any' work, sickness benefit would cease.

3 Ethical issues regarding long-term sick notes. Consider own position concerning long-term sickness benefit, and also whether or not agreement would help the patient's outcome in the long term.

9.4

Your next patient, Sarah Spencer, is a woman of 45 who consults you regularly about an anxiety state. On this occasion she tells you that something she worries about a lot is that her mother died of Huntington's chorea. How would you advise her?

CONSTRUCTS

1 The facts about Huntington's inheritance. Find out how much the patient knows about Huntington's chorea and its inheritance. Explain, if necessary, that it is a progressive condition leading to dementia and death. Patient's chances of inheriting the disease if her mother had it are 1 in 2. There is no effective treatment as yet, although one day there may be.

2 The pros of testing. The gene can be detected with reasonable accuracy. A negative result will allay anxiety. The patient will also be in a position to advise her children of any risk to them.

3 The cons of testing. A positive result will not help as far as treatment is concerned and may considerably increase anxiety. Possible problems with life insurance and mortgages.

4 Autonomy. Counselling within the practice and elsewhere. The decision to test or not is for the patient, but doctors should help by providing full information and being prepared to discuss the issues. The possibility of using outside agencies, e.g. local genetic counselling unit.

9.5

At coffee time you are visited by a representative from a pharmaceutical company who asks if you would like to attend a scientific meeting in Nice. Your expenses would be reimbursed. The meeting appears to be legitimate and the subject interests you. What issues does this invitation raise?

CONSTRUCTS

1 Legal issues. Are you allowed to accept the drug company's hospitality? Be aware of the legal position. A doctor is allowed to accept such an invitation provided that the level of hospitality is not excessive and the offer is not an inducement to prescribe.

2 Ethical issues. Should you accept such an offer? Although perfectly legal, the arrangement may appear a little dubious. However, in industry and commerce this kind of activity is routine.

3 Consequences of accepting. Under an obligation: the rep may feel that he has done the doctor a favour and may expect the doctor to reciprocate by seeing the rep on a regular basis or by prescribing the drugs made by the company.

4 Educational issues. The problem of who should pay for continuing education: doctors mostly don't want to and the pharmaceutical industry may have ulterior motives.

9.6

A 35-year-old schoolteacher, Paul Wright, presents with a 4-day history of cough, wheeze and copious green sputum. There is no significant past history and on examination he has expiratory rhonchi but no signs of consolidation. Outline and explain your management.

CONSTRUCTS

1 Further investigation considered. PEF useful, chest X-ray and sputum culture probably not much help.

2 Diagnostic possibilities. Patient may have asthma and/or acute bronchitis. Not possible at this stage to know which.

3 Treatment. If PEF down, use of inhaled beta-adrenergic would be appropriate; if PEF down to < 60% oral steroids. Most general practitioners would consider prescribing an antibiotic as well, although doubtful if strictly necessary. Amoxycillin or erythromycin use should be considered.

4 Follow-up. Patient should be reviewed in 1–2 weeks – ideally with peak-flow chart to see if it is asthma – for specific purposes of full diagnosis and decisions about further treatment.

9.7

Naomi Moss, a 25-year-old hairdresser, asks for a supply of acyclovir cream, to treat recurrent cold sores. How would you respond?

CONSTRUCTS

1 Discussion. Adult – patient's views should be treated with respect – a non-confrontational approach. Naomi's views on acyclovir for herpes simplex should be listened to and explored.

2 Diagnosis. Is Naomi right in her diagnosis? Could it be something else? Take appropriate steps to confirm the diagnosis by history and examination.

3 Significance. Is it bad enough to treat? Explore the effect of the problem on Naomi's life. Does it happen frequently? Does it cause problems with her job, which obviously involves the public?

4 Treatment. Discuss with Naomi the appropriateness or otherwise of prescribing, based on the effects of the problem and the resource implications. If prescribing does not appear to be justified, Naomi could be advised on the possible OTC purchase of acyclovir.

9.8

After surgery you visit Andy Smith, a 56-year-old man you recently referred to the chest physicians. He has been discharged after investigation with a diagnosis of terminal bronchogenic carcinoma. Mrs Smith asks to speak to you alone for a moment. She tells you that Andy does not know the diagnosis and she asks you not to tell him the truth as it would surely kill him. How would you respond?

CONSTRUCTS

1 Empathy. Mrs Smith trying to be kind. She has had a shock herself. How is she bearing up? Express sympathy, ask after her own state of health, allow her to express her concerns and fears.

2 Autonomy. Explain, as gently as possible, that Mr Smith is entitled to the truth if he wants to hear it. He may wish to tidy up his affairs in the time left or to carry out some unfulfilled plans. Would be unethical for a doctor to withhold this information; none of us can arrogate to ourselves the right to decide what another adult should or should not be told in the situation.

3 The right not to know. Explain that he/she will certainly not force the truth on Mr Smith. It would be normal for Mr Smith to ask about the diagnosis. If he does not ask, the doctor may offer the opportunity to Mr Smith to raise the issue. If the issue is not raised, the doctor will assume that Mr Smith suspects the truth but does not wish it to be confirmed.

4 Honesty or collusion. Explain that maintaining the pretence that all will be well can be very difficult, particularly when Mr Smith may well know the truth and be doing the same thing for her.

5 A positive approach. Emphasize the advantages of sharing the future together and being able to talk to each other about fears and concerns. Mr Smith will also be able to share with the doctor fears of dying in pain, etc. The doctor will be able to reassure Mr Smith that this will not happen.

9.9

Harry Jones, a 19-year-old student, presents on his return from spending a year-out backpacking in the Far East. He complains of weight loss and general malaise. What possible problems might account for this and what initial investigations would you carry out?

CONSTRUCTS

1 Infectious disease. Mention the wide range of infections and infestations possible. Also cover STD infections such as hepatitis B and HIV.

2 Other physical causes. Consider a wide range of other physical causes, such as diabetes, leukaemia, lymphoma, etc.

3 Nutritional problems. Consider the possibility of poor nutrition during the year-out as being of possible relevance.

4 Psychiatric/emotional problems. Consider the possibility of psychiatric problems. Stress of being away for a year, the problems of trying to fit back into an academic life, the right age-group for several psychiatric problems.

5 Investigations. Suggest doing a preliminary set of screening blood tests, such as FBC, ESR and biochemical screen. Depending on the results of this screen, would then move on to more extensive testing.

9.10

Your long-serving practice manager tells you that she intends to retire in 3 months. The partners decide that you should draw up a 'person profile' of the appropriate replacement. Outline the features that would make up the profile of a practice manager.

CONSTRUCTS

1 Personal qualities. Suggest that the ideal candidate should be self-motivating, diplomatic, determined and thorough.

2 Skills. Suggest that skills in management, team building, computing and accountancy would be appropriate.

3 Experience and background. Suggest that appropriate experience would be in a management or administrative capacity, ideally involving working with the public.

4 Qualifications. Suggest that some form of business management qualification would be appropriate, mention that there are specific diplomas for practice managers.

5 Equal opportunities. Do not include in the profile any preferences as to age, gender, race.

Commentary 9

The surgery deals with some 'bread-and-butter' general practice, e.g. infrequent periods and diarrhoea, but also presents more major conditions, e.g. asthma, bronchial carcinoma. It also looks at some of the conflicts facing the general practitioner, e.g. advertising and employing staff. The constructs in this surgery include prescribing for friends, mixing work with friends, practical therapeutics, the ethical issues of sick notes, genetic counselling, funding of education, consequences of accepting gifts, honesty or collusion, nutritional problems and personal qualities.

MEQ 10

Just before you are due to start morning surgery you are asked to see Calum Davidson, a 46-year-old man who has presented at reception with chest pain. From the history it becomes clear that Mr Davidson is having an MI. Outline your management.

CONSTRUCTS

1 Immediate management of MI. Explain the diagnosis to Mr Davidson, check that there are no contraindications to normal management. Give i.v. analgesia, e.g. 5 mg i.v. diamorphine slowly, and an aspirin.

2 Immediate management of any complications. Check the patient for left ventricular failure, tachycardia or bradycardia, and if any are present manage appropriately.

3 Long-term management. Explain to Mr Davidson what is happening and give him an idea of what will happen in coronary care. Explain that follow-up will be necessary once Mr Davidson gets home, but that a return to normal life can be expected.

4 Practicalities. Organize an immediate ambulance and alert the coronary care unit that the patient is on the way in. Consider whether or not to travel with the patient in the ambulance. Once the rush is over, arrange for Mrs Davidson to be informed and also make sure that the patients kept waiting have been given a reason for the delay.

10.2

Your first booked patient of the day is Mrs Jane Stone, a 73-year-old widow. She tells you that, on the advice of her son, a physician in the USA, she has come for a cholesterol check. How would you respond?

CONSTRUCTS

1 Count to ten. Recognize that you are stressed – just dealt with an emergency, running late, and Mrs Stone's reasons for consulting may irritate. A brief pause for reflection to avoid responding too harshly.

2 Prevention. Comment to Mrs Stone that it is important that she is thinking about her long-term health and welcome her interest.

3 The agenda. Ask Mrs Stone about the reasons for her son's suggestion, enquire about family history and any other factors which may have prompted her request.

4 The facts. Explain that there is no evidence that treating raised cholesterol is useful in this age-group, and that drugs can have significant side-effects.

5 Negotiation. Suggest to Mrs Stone that a cholesterol check would not be helpful. If she still wishes to have the test after this discussion, it will be carried out.

10.3

Your next patient is 7-year-old Tom Turner, who attends with his mother, Sharon, for a routine review of his asthma. He is currently using salbutamol via a large-volume spacer device as needed. What criteria would you use to decide on further management?

CONSTRUCTS

1 Quality of life. Look at the areas of time off school, frequency of symptoms, nocturnal wakening, limiting of activities. If any of these events are happening, consider adding prophylaxis.

2 Salbutamol usage. Find out how often Tom needs to use his salbutamol. If use is more than once per day, consider adding prophylaxis.

3 Views of Sharon and Tom. Ask mother and child how they feel about the asthma control and how convenient Tom finds the spacer.

4 Theoretical concepts. Aggressive use of prophylaxis may produce a reduction in the long-term severity of the disease.

5 Overall decision. Based on all of the above, consider the following options: stopping all treatment, changing the device to a more convenient one, i.e. MDI or dry-powder device, or adding prophylaxis with inhaled steroid or cromoglycate.

10.4

Your next patient is George Hagan, a 52-year-old bank clerk, who is attending as a result of a new-patient medical, at which your practice nurse measured his BP at 146/104. There is no significant past or current history. Outline your management plan.

CONSTRUCTS

1 Explanation and discussion. Explain to Mr Hagan that he may have high BP but that it will be some time before you can be sure. State that this will not cause symptoms or ill health in the short term, but if confirmed could result in long-term problems – stroke, heart attack, etc. Therefore need for monitoring and advisability of treatment if diagnosis confirmed.

2 Monitoring. Check BP today and if diastolic still between 90 and 110 arrange for follow-up measurements over next 3 months until/unless readings move outside range. May use practice nurse for follow-up.

3 Investigations. Examine the patient at this visit – fundi, heart. Eventual investigations would include urine testing. ECG, biochemical screening, cholesterol.

4 Treatment. Initial non-drug management – diet, alcohol, exercise – followed if necessary by drug treatment, e.g. 2.5 mg bendrofluazide, beta-blocker or ACEI as first line. Concept of trying to tailor treatment to individual patient.

5 Long-term follow-up. Discuss the need for long-term follow-up and agree to this with patient. BP review every 3 months at first and then probably every 6 months. Emphasis on patient responsibility for follow-up. Discuss need for practice tracking and recall system.

10.5

At coffee time your practice manager mentions that the staff were concerned that your first patient, Mr Davidson, had looked quite unwell in the waiting-room. The staff members felt they would not have known what to do if he had collapsed. What issues does this raise for the practice?

CONSTRUCTS

1 Emergency plan for practice. Acknowledge that the practice should have written guidelines for staff for this kind of occasion, including how to contact duty doctor, when to phone for an ambulance, etc.

2 Staff training. Staff members should be trained in first aid and CPR. Also consider CPR retraining for doctors in the practice.

3 Health and safety issues. Consider the Health and Safety at Work Act and the possible legal requirement to train staff in first aid and CPR.

4 Equipment. Review the provision and maintainance of resuscitation equipment in the practice. The pros and cons of having a defibrillator and intubation facilities.

10.6

Your next patient is Jane Hepburn, a 34-year-old woman, who complains of a sore face. When you examine her, it becomes clear that the cause is a carious tooth with a large cavity. Mrs Hepburn readily agrees with this diagnosis and tells you that she has come to you rather than the dentist because the dentist wants £30 to see her. Outline your management.

CONSTRUCTS

1 Horses for courses. The problem is dental and a dentist would be best placed to advise. Explain this to Mrs Hepburn. Possibility of surgical treatment, dentist able to prescribe antibiotics.

2 Finance. Explore the possibility of financial help – bring in other agencies – social work, etc.

3 Treatment. Provide immediate treatment while still advising dental help. Treatment along the lines of amoxycillin plus metronidazole, with advice on analgesia and drug side-effects.

4 General action. Raise this issue with partners and possibly with FSHA and LMC. Doctors should not be in the position of supplying general dental services.

10.7

Your next patient, 19-year-old Audrey Fonda, bursts into tears when she enters the room. When she calms down, she tells you that she has just broken off her engagement and wishes to cancel her honeymoon trip due in 5 months' time. The travel agent has told her she will lose her deposit unless she can obtain a letter from her doctor to enable her to cancel on medical grounds. How would you handle this request?

CONSTRUCTS

1 Sensitivity. Express sympathy with Ms Fonda's situation. Allow her time to vent her feelings. Do not produce an immediate response.

2 Possible medical problems. Ascertain that the patient, although upset, is not clinically depressed. Also confirm that there are no medical implications involved in the reasons for the split – e.g. promiscuity, violence, etc.

3 Writing the letter. Explain that a letter could only be written if there was a medical problem which would preclude travel. Even if the young woman appears depressed at this point, it is extremely unlikely that she will still be depressed in 5 months' time. Seek patient's understanding of this.

4 Long-term relationship. This consultation could have effects on the long-term relationship with this patient. The young woman is a candidate for depression or stress-related illness in the medium term. Leave the door open for a return appointment if necessary.

10.8

Your next patient is Kurt Conham, a 25-year-old man, whom you know to have a long history of substance abuse. He brings a letter from the local drug abuse centre which asks you to prescribe long-term methadone. The letter is signed by a 'counsellor'. Discuss the implications of this request.

CONSTRUCTS

1 The individual patient. The pros and cons of maintenance therapy – the harm reduction model.

2 Practice implications. Influx of drug-abusers, staff harassment, security implications.

3 Practice co-ordination. The practice as a whole needs to discuss and review systems for management of drug-users and policies to deal with them.

4 Co-ordination with drug centres. Need to get together with drug centre to thrash out the referral rules, formulate a common policy and establish a named individual, preferably a doctor, to liaise with the practice.

10.9

Your next patient, Diana Ferguson, who is a cook, attends for review after an episode of gastroenteritis. She was first seen by a partner in the practice 2 weeks ago. After a swab apparently grew *Helicobacter*, she was advised to stay off work until a negative specimen was obtained. Her second specimen is negative but, while telling her this, you notice that her first specimen was also negative; the *Helicobacter* swab related to a previous episode. What would you do?

CONSTRUCTS

1 Should you admit to a mix-up? Discuss the options – possible anger from patient at losing time from work if the truth is told, problem of what to do next if nothing is said.

2 Advice to patient. Advise the patient that she is now safe to return to work and discuss ways of avoiding infection in the future.

3 Examine the system. Examine the report filing system to see if the mistake was purely human error or whether an alternative system of recording might be helpful.

4 Speak to colleague. Discuss the issue with the colleague involved – non-confrontational approach. Consider operating a significant event analysis on a regular basis.

10.10

Your prescribing adviser points out that your practice is spending a lot on ranitidine. The practice commissions you to produce a plan to reduce this spending. Discuss how you might make savings.

CONSTRUCTS

1 Indications for H_2 blockers. Discuss the possibility of a protocol for the management of dyspepsia and reflux, in which H_2 blockers appear at an agreed point in the protocol. Discuss the need for ownership, agreement and monitoring for a set of guidelines to work.

2 Alternative cheaper drugs. Point out that ranitidine is considerably more expensive than generic cimetidine – potential problems with interactions, but these are very unusual.

3 *Helicobacter* **eradication.** Consider the possibility of *Helicobacter* eradication in ulcer patients as a way of reducing spending: 90% of DU patients have *H. pylori* and eradication will provide a long-term cure and reduction in prescribing.

4 Lifestyle interventions. Consider the idea of using health education more to try to reduce the need for H_2 prescribing. This is effective but compliance is not easy. Compliance with lifestyle advice would have side-benefits in terms of reduction in smoking and obesity.

Commentary 10

The surgery includes an acute situation and the subsequent consequences for the staff. It also highlights the easy accessibility of the general practitioner when he is presented with problems which should go to other health professionals. The financial accountability is highlighted with a visit from the prescribing adviser. The constructs include prescribing negotiation, quality of life, theoretical concepts, monitoring, emergency planning, staff training, health and safety issues, sensitivity, co-ordination with drug centre and lifestyle intervention.

MEQ 11

You receive a message from a local gynaecologist informing you that Michaela Kelly, who is 11 weeks postpartum, was admitted the previous night by the deputizing doctor with heavy vaginal bleeding. She was discharged within 24 hours but her scan result is now to hand and shows a large vascular cystic area in the uterus, aetiology unknown. Under no circumstances should she have a D and C if further bleeding occurs. How would you respond to this?

CONSTRUCTS

1 Action needed. Important that this information should be disseminated to all doctors who may be looking after this patient.

2 Patient needs. Importance of knowing patient's current condition, her treatment, accessibility to telephone in an emergency and what arrangements are in place for the baby should admission be required.

3 Patient knowledge. Identifies what the patient has been told and whether she has a stipulated plan of action should further bleeding occur.

4 Protocol. Awareness of the benefit of a set action plan which is known by the patient, doctors and receptionist, with a copy in the patient notes.

5 Communication. Highlights the importance of quality information from the hospital and good communication between the deputizing service and the practice about hospital referrals.

11.2

Andrina Morrison is a 35-year-old woman who suffers from MS. She has recently read about the use of interferon in this disease and would like to know if, as a fundholding practice, you could prescribe this for her.

CONSTRUCTS

1 Knowledge of drug. Identifies the importance of knowing about the effect of this drug in MS, what trials have been reported, the possible side-effects and where to find out such information.

2 Limits in competence. Is willing to admit to the patient a lack of knowledge but is able to identify ways of addressing these knowledge gaps.

3 Cost. Is aware of cost implications of fundholding practices and whether this would be included in the budget or allowed for by prescribing adviser.

4 Ethics. Discusses the ethical dilemma in treating patients with expensive treatment on a fundholding budget.

5 Doctor/patient relationship. Realizes the importance of maintaining the doctor/patient relationship when the request for specific treatment may have to be turned down.

11.3

Nancy Nisbet is the elderly mother of one of your patients who has recently been diagnosed with breast cancer and bony secondaries. The mother is not your patient but she is keen to have more information about the diagnosis and prognosis as the family have given her no details and she wants to help to look after her daughter. How would you deal with this request?

CONSTRUCTS

1 Confidentiality. Shows awareness that the doctor is bound by the rules of confidentiality to the patient and importance of having the patient's consent before divulging information.

2 Patient knowledge. Important to identify the patient's views about divulging information to the mother and establishing what the patient knows about the condition.

3 Family relationships. Importance of family dynamics and why the family are withholding information; may not want mother's help. Encourages mother to talk to daughter and family.

4 Mother's knowledge. Establishes what the mother already knows and tries to identify what she sees as her role. Is she physically and emotionally capable of looking after a dying relative?

5 Nursing support. Tries to identify any nursing needs the patient may have. Shows awareness of the pros and cons of using an outside agency rather than family support.

11.4

Mary Burns comes with her 11-month-old daughter for the results of a second urine test which was requested by your partner. The previous MSSU was reported as showing enterococcal ? significance and the repeat test has given the same result. How would you proceed?

CONSTRUCTS

1 Diagnosis. Is aware of the need to review symptoms, presentations and clinical examination since not seen by you but by another partner.

2 Mother/child relationship. Is aware of importance of assessing the child/mother interaction and the child's behaviour.

3 Hidden agenda. Is aware that it could be the mother who has the problem and not the child. ? Psychiatric illness in the mother.

4 Sample collection. Shows awareness of the difficulty of obtaining MSSU in children. Gives explanation of sterile techniques for children.

5 Referral. Is aware of the indications for referral for UTI in children and the impact of this on child and mother.

11.5

Mrs Deirdre Ferguson is a 64-year-old woman who joined your practice 1 year ago. She has had her new-patient interview with the practice nurse and saw one of your partners 6 months previously for a repeat prescription of Premarin (unconjugated oestrogen). This had been started by her previous general practitioner 12 years before. She is requesting a further 6-monthly prescription but, on questioning her, you discover that she has not had a hysterectomy. What issues does this raise?

CONSTRUCTS

1 Patient management. Is aware of the risk of unopposed oestrogen in non-hysterectomized women and the effects on the patient should it now be stopped. Should raise possibility of referral for D and C and should assess the ongoing need for HRT and possibility of changing to a more suitable therapy.

2 Communication. Should be aware of the sensitive nature of the information being delivered and consider ways of doing this. Should be aware of the importance for honesty.

3 Practice implications. Does the practice nurse need further training? Should there be an audit of care of menopausal women in the practice? Should there be a protocol for care developed?

4 Partner relationships. Should address the issue of speaking to the partner who previously prescribed the drug. Is there a need for updating of knowledge in the medical staff?

5 Legal issues. Threat of litigation as a result of inappropriate treatment or difficulty in criticizing a colleague. Should raise the issue of whether other doctor should be contacted.

6 Doctor/patient relationship. Shows awareness of the impact of the information on the patient and the effect it may have on the relationship with your partner.

11.6

A 17-year-old Asian girl, Brenda Prasad, requests the morning-after pill. She has had two similar consultations with other doctors in the practice. What areas would you like to cover?

CONSTRUCTS

1 Patient beliefs. Should show importance of determining the patient's knowledge of contraception and views. Any contraindications to contraception, any religious or cultural objections? Fear of lack of confidentiality.

2 Risk-taking behaviour. Should highlight the risks of unprotected intercourse, i.e. risk of pregnancy, STDs, multiple partners, HIV. Is she taking drugs?

3 Social. Importance of determining the family status and relationship with parents, whether they know of the relationship and if she is living at home.

4 Management. Which contraceptive to use, number of times morning-after pill can be prescribed, prevention such as cervical smear, vaginal swabs and LMPs.

5 Doctor/patient relationship. Importance of establishing rapport for continuity of care, emphasis on seeing one doctor only and importance of not being judgemental.

11.7

Pauline McKay, an unmarried 37-year-old, has been attending you with complaints of menorrhagia and severe dysmenorrhoea. She has been fully investigated by a gynaecologist, who has found no abnormality but has advised hysterectomy. She has appeared with her mother to discuss this with you. How would you proceed?

CONSTRUCTS

1 Diagnosis. Shows awareness of the implication of a hysterectomy when no diagnosis has been made. Possibility of other reasons for symptoms.

2 Patient's views. Has patient been involved in this decision-making? Is the patient pushing to have this carried out? Is she aware of the implications of the treatment?

3 Long-term effect. Aware of the effect on fertility and psyche and problems if it does not relieve symptoms; also the impact on future relationships and possible marriage for the patient.

4 Family dynamics. Who is the patient – mother or daughter? What is the relationship?

5 Communication with colleagues. Need to contact consultant to obtain his views and reason for treatment. Is not afraid to question consultant's decisions and puts patient's interests first.

11.8

Gordon White is a 33-year-old infrequent attender who complains of intermittent weakness in his arms over the last few months. Recently he has dropped things on one or two occasions and thinks he may be stressed at work. How would you deal with this complaint?

CONSTRUCTS

1 Establish diagnosis. Shows awareness of the need to reach diagnosis and, although symptoms are unusual, the possibility is that it may be a serious underlying organic disease, e.g. MS. ? Psychological. Able to give appropriate investigations and possible referral.

2 Communication. Shows empathy with patient and explains fully the implications of possible diagnoses in a sensitive manner.

3 Psychological assessment. Important to define what is meant by being stressed at work and to gain an outline of the patient's lifestyle.

4 Management. Explores the possibility of a need for psychotropic drugs to alleviate patient's stress.

11.9

Gary McQueen, 33, asks for a 1-week course of Nizoral tablets. He had a similar prescription 3 weeks ago but claims the chemist only had enough to dispense a 5-day supply. His skin condition has not improved and, since it was not his fault that he failed to complete the first course, he is refusing to pay for this prescription and demands that either you or the chemist does so. How would you deal with this situation?

CONSTRUCTS

1 Correct prescription. Establishes the correct diagnosis was made and the appropriate prescription was given. Is another treatment more appropriate, is a cheaper treatment as acceptable?

2 Chemist's view. Establishes facts from the chemist's point of view: do they have inappropriate stock or was the balance of tablets not collected by the patient?

3 Patient responsibility. Shows awareness that it is the responsibility of the patient to complete the course of treatment and to pay for the cost of prescription.

4 Cost implications. Shows awareness of the cost of prescribing a second course of treatment. Considers a cheaper alternative.

11.10

The final patient of the day is an emergency who complains of a painful eye. Your receptionist informs you that he had been in surgery earlier in the day demanding to be seen but the appointment given then had been unsuitable. He had gone to casualty but it had been too busy for him to wait and he has now appeared at the surgery once more. How would you deal with this man?

CONSTRUCTS

1 Clinical condition. The importance of dealing with the clinical problem in the first instance. Aware that there are possible serious conditions that may cause a painful eye and of the possible treatments of these.

2 Patient beliefs. Exposes the patient's anxiety about his condition. Aware that there may be other underlying reasons to justify his behaviour in the surgery. Was he aware of the appointments system within the surgery?

3 Patient behaviour. Shows willingness to confront patient with behaviour and not afraid to point out when behaviour is inappropriate.

4 Practice implications. Importance of having staff trained to deal with a difficult patient. The importance of good communication so that all patients know how the appointments system works.

Commentary 11

This surgery has a high number of gynaecological problems and problems affecting females. This could be related to a female doctor or a doctor with a particular interest in this area. In addition to this, skills are required in other areas and these can be seen from the other patients presented. The constructs include action need and protocol, limits in competence, nursing support, mother-and-child relationship, hidden agenda, partners' relationship, risk-taking behaviour, communication with colleagues, psychological assessment and chemist's view.

MEQ 12

Iona Smith brings her 10-year-old son Ian to the surgery with a small verruca on the sole of his foot. She asks for a letter excusing him from sports until it resolves. How would you deal with this?

CONSTRUCTS

1 Explanation. Aware of natural history of the disease and the importance of explanation.

2 Management. Outlines appropriate treatment options.

3 Prevention. Aware of importance of advice on avoiding spread to others and recurrence.

4 Mother's fears. Importance of exploring mother's fears – absence from sport is overreaction to diagnosis.

5 School problems. ? Underachievement at sport. ? Bullying. ? School phobia.

12.2

Willie McCann telephones the surgery complaining of a sore throat for 2 days, not helped by aspirin gargles. He is going abroad that evening and is unable to come to the surgery. What action would you take?

CONSTRUCTS

1 Telephone advice. Aware of the difficulties in giving advice over the telephone.

2 Prescription. Discusses the implication of giving antibiotics and justifies decision and treatment.

3 Patient expectation. Is aware that this may set the pattern of behaviour for this patient. Has he done this before?

4 Practice policy. Discusses value of policy on prescribing antibiotics over the telephone.

5 Appointment system. Importance of system which is flexible enough to accommodate emergency, i.e. can patient genuinely not come down or are there no appointments?

12.3

The practice holds a meeting to discuss changing your out-of-hours cover from an extended rota with a neighbouring practice to using deputizing. What aspects must the practice consider?

CONSTRUCTS

1 Patient care. Raises issue of continuity of care, patient preference and monitoring quality of care provided by deputizing.

2 Workload. Explores benefits of working hard by day but not at night, amount of deputizing to be used, other alternatives to deputizing, e.g. locums.

3 Finance. Explores cost/benefit of employing a deputizing agency.

4 Effect on other practice. Option now for neighbouring doctors with increased rota: will they attract patients from them?

5 Communication. Importance of relaying information on patients visited.

6 Doctor responsibility. Aware that doctors have 24-hour responsibility and are legally responsible for the deputies' actions.

12.4

Mrs Ashraf Patel, a 53-year-old frequent attender, telephones the surgery complaining of epigastric pain. She is given advice and 30 minutes later you are called urgently to the house as she has collapsed. On arrival you find Mrs Patel dead. What problems confront you?

CONSTRUCTS

1 Relative reaction. Outlines responses and hostility likely to encounter.

2 Communication. Aware of difficulty of language barrier.

3 Cultural. Importance of respecting religious rites to examining body, burial, etc.

4 Sudden death. Aware of procedures surrounding sudden death of patient.

5 Doctor/patient relationship. Aware of implication of this scenario on long-term relationship with family.

12.5

Frances Black, 32, comes to you complaining of weight gain since starting Provera for menorrhagia. She requests a prescription for Tenuate Dospan, which her sister had been prescribed by her own doctor with great success. How do you respond to this?

CONSTRUCTS

1 Establish symptoms. Importance of assessing weight gain. Explore other causes, e.g. diet or eating disorder.

2 Alternative therapy. Explores the possibility of changing hormone therapy, gives diet advice.

3 Cost/benefit. Highlights cost in terms of side-effects of appetite suppressants vs. dubious short-term benefits.

4 Criticism of colleague. Aware of difficulties in being seen to criticize sister's doctor.

5 Health care team. Sees opportunity to involve practice nurse.

12.6

Marlene Dempsey contacts the surgery requesting a prescription for her 4-year-old son John, who is 'chesty'. You manage to call her back later in the day with the intention of seeing the child at the surgery. Mrs Dempsey informs you that all is well as your health visitor called earlier with a prescription for Amoxil. What issues does this raise?

CONSTRUCTS

1 Absent patient. Discusses dilemma of giving patients prescriptions without being seen.

2 Prescription. Raises issue of who wrote prescription: was this an appropriate treatment?

3 Patient expectation. Aware that this response may set precedent for this mother in future.

4 Communication. Discusses the importance of patient contacts and treatments being entered in notes.

5 Health visitor. Defines role of health visitor and limits of competence, lack of expertise in clinical assessment.

6 Doctor behaviour. Realizes importance of defining reasons behind doctor issuing prescription.

7 Confrontation. Highlights importance of confronting doctor and health visitor with actions.

8 Litigation. Aware of risks of litigation should anything go wrong.

12.7

Maria Ross, a 28-year-old business executive, is 2 months post-partum. She is breast-feeding her first child and is concerned and upset because he vomits after every feed. How would you deal with this?

CONSTRUCTS

1 Establish symptoms and diagnosis. Importance of defining presenting complaint and thinks of appropriate diagnoses.

2 Examination. Importance of examining child and monitor weight.

3 Mother's attitude. Explores mother's feelings re breast-feeding.

4 Hidden agenda. Who is patient – mother or baby? Is it an excuse to stop breast-feeding, is she depressed, does she wish to return to work?

5 PHCT. Considers involving health visitor for support.

12.8

Your practice nurse decides that she would like to start a travel clinic in the surgery. What implications does this have for the practice?

CONSTRUCTS

1 Nurse training. Aware of importance of proper training and competence.

2 Finance. Cost to practice and income generation.

3 Time and space. Impact on rescheduling timetable to accommodate new clinic. ? Lose other appointments.

4 Advertising. Aware of the rules surrounding advertising services via local travel agents, etc.

5 Assessment of need. Looks at work in practice to determine the demand for such a clinic.

12.9

Mrs Linda Thomson, 50, enters your surgery and bursts into tears. She has discovered that her husband has been having an affair with a younger woman. She has not slept for a week and is very distraught. How would you help her?

CONSTRUCTS

1 Show understanding. Shows the importance of showing sympathy and empathy for the patient's situation.

2 Patient's feelings. Explores how patient feels and implications for the future.

3 Drug treatment. Considers whether the patient requires antidepressants/anxiolytics and mentions appropriate drugs in this situation.

4 Social circumstances. Shows awareness of the importance of determining social circumstances, family support, children, financial circumstances.

5 Legal implications. Is aware of advising the patient on importance of determining their legal rights.

6 Outside agencies. Is aware of support agencies and counselling agencies available, e.g. marriage guidance.

12.10

A 74-year-old anxious woman, Stella Hillis, who is a frequent attender, is visibly upset about a consultation 2 days before with a locum doctor, who she claims was rude and aggressive towards her. She wishes to complain but is afraid you will put her off your list if she does so. How would you respond to this?

CONSTRUCTS

1 **Communication.** Importance of listening to the patient and establishing facts and define rude and aggressive.

2 **Show understanding.** Importance of sympathizing with the patient and trying to restore confidence in the doctor/patient relationship. Reassurance that this is not something for which you would remove her from your list.

3 **Patient management.** Is there an underlying anxiety/psychiatric problem which requires further treatment? Give examples of these and ways in which to treat this.

4 **Patient's complaint.** Is the complaint justified? Does the patient still wish to go forward with the complaint and if so does the patient know how to do this?

5 **Practice implications.** Is there a policy for auditing the quality of locum work? Are locums necessary in the practice and is there a complaints procedure for patients to follow?

6 **Action needed.** Prepares to speak to locum doctor to hear the doctor's version of events. Is this a recurring problem? Does this doctor need help?

Commentary 12

The surgery dealt with a range of problems, related both to everyday problems in general practice and to more difficult life events. The surgery also dealt with problems of out-of-hours calls and the question of innovation, e.g. travel clinic. The constructs include mothers' fears, school problems, telephone advice, workload, cultural, criticism of colleague, absent patient, confrontation, advertising, nurse training and outside agencies.

MEQ 13

Assume you are in a suburban, five-partner practice which has a full complement of ancillary staff and is non-fundholding.

13.1

Roger Turner, a 42-year-old accountant, comes to see you requesting referral for homoeopathic treatment. He has been suffering from headaches for some time and has been fully investigated by your partner but no cause has been found. What factors might influence your decision regarding the suitability of referral?

CONSTRUCTS

1 Reassessment of patient. Elimination of undiagnosed cause, history, repeat physical examination (fundi, BP, sinuses, cervical spine, etc.). Assess mental state.

2 Patient's beliefs and expectations. Open consulting style, fears of serious pathology, e.g. brain tumour, understanding of uses/benefits, mode of action, of homoeopathic treatment. Emphasis on process as well as content.

3 Respect for patient's needs. Understanding of reaction to dissatisfaction with conventional medicine, peer pressure/adverts, etc. Need to do something positive.

4 Doctor's feelings. Annoyance/frustration re second opinion, loss of control, sharing responsibility for patient care, uncertainty re unproved treatment, risk of colleagues' criticism.

5 Organizational/administrative aspects. Referral and availabilty privately/on NHS, extracontractual referrals, prescribing of homoeopathic medicines.

13.2

Martha Owen, a 48-year-old teacher consults you with symptoms of flushing, night sweats and anxiety. She says her periods have become irregular and scanty over the past 6 months and insists that HRT would help her. What factors would influence your response to her request?

CONSTRUCTS

1 Suitability for treatment. Family history, menstrual history, PMH, contraindications to HRT, negative physical exam, mental state, compliance and follow-up.

2 Assessment of symptoms. Full history and examination, differential diagnosis to include organic and psychological diagnoses, e.g. menopause, dysfunctional uterine bleeding, thyroid dysfunction, depression, etc.

3 Patient's expectations. Sources of information, expectations of HRT to give symptom relief, prevention of osteoporosis, relief of depression, etc. Benefits and side-effects.

4 Patient's insistence on treatment. Reasons for this – mentions personality, severity of symptoms, peer pressure, hidden agenda.

5 Communication issues. Discusses options in open manner.

6 Reaching decision. Is there evidence of logical approach to decision-making?

13.3

The personnel officer of a local TV company (to whom you are medical adviser) phones you to ask for advice about the content of first-aid kits to be carried in company cars. What advice would you give?

CONSTRUCTS

1 Function of kits. Who would use them, range of use depending on skills of those using them, supervision of use.

2 Contents of kits. Essential contents – gloves, airways, bandages, splints, etc. Prepacked kits vs. 'home-made', where to purchase. ? Profit for practice.

3 Reason for request. Recent accident, media propaganda, union pressure, inadequate ambulance facilities.

4 Doctor's role. Involvement in training, opportunity to extend training in first aid, exertion of political pressure, fee-earning for practice.

13.4

One of your partners suggests that the practice opens a Sunday surgery to relieve the on-call work at weekends. What issues does this raise?

CONSTRUCTS

1 Assessment of need. Analysis of weekend workload, patient demand, feasibility.

2 Implications for Partnership. Mentions doctors, receptionists, patients, resources.

3 Reasons for partner's suggestion. Mentions 'burn-out', dislike of home visits, safety, patient/spouse pressure.

4 Partnership dynamics. Relationships between partners, practice policy, organization, how decisions are reached.

5 Wider issues. Security, raising patient expectations, financial implications, implications for staff.

13.5

Mrs Higginson brings her 5-year-old daughter, Harriet, to you. She is very worried because she saw some droplets of blood on Harriet's pants last night. What issues might this consultation raise?

CONSTRUCTS

1 Mother's fears, concerns and expectations. Concern re diagnosis, serious illness, sexual abuse, other abuse, suspects within the family, medicolegal implications, infections.

2 Doctor's concerns. Diagnosis, uncertainty, lack of expertise, suspicion of sexual abuse, awareness of family dynamics, decision to involve outside agencies, e.g. police, social services, etc., relationship with Harriet and her parents, difficulties of examination, reluctance to get involved.

3 Harriet's feelings. Fear of examination, past experiences, fear of doctor, embarrassment.

4 Establishment of diagnosis. Establishment of rapport with Harriet, observation of child – mother relationship, general examination, examination of perineum, swabs, foreign bodies, urine.

5 Management. Involvement of other agencies, advice, appropriate management after diagnosis, education of mother, adequate explanation, referral.

13.6

Mrs Driscoll attends surgery to tell you that she thinks she is pregnant. She is 38 and this is her first pregnancy. She has been on phenytoin to control her grand-mal seizures for some years. What advice would you want to give her?

CONSTRUCTS

1 General health. Smoking, alcohol, exercise, diet, foods to avoid, dental care, medication, smear.

2 Phenytoin therapy. Risks to fetus and mother, decision to stop or continue and who makes the decision, informed consent, sources of advice, positive attitude.

3 Pregnancy advice. Confirmation of pregnancy, shared care, home vs. hospital delivery, routine care including screening, folic acid, benefits available.

4 Age. Positive attitude, risks, amniocentesis/chorionic villous biopsy.

5 Epilepsy. Effect of pregnancy, effect on fetus, mode of inheritance, effect of medication.

13.7

Miss Powell, an 85-year-old woman with cataracts, attends your surgery for the third time in 3 months requesting that her admission for cataract surgery be expedited. She asks if she would be better off in a fundholding practice. What issues does this raise?

CONSTRUCTS

1 Doctor's role. Clinical need assessor, patient's advocate, gatekeeper of resources, maintenance of doctor–patient relationship.

2 Patient's concerns/expectations. Fear of blindness, anxiety re increase in symptoms, fear of surgery, anxiety re outcome of treatment, not reassured by doctors, previous experiences, knowledge of Patient's Charter.

3 Doctor's feelings. Anger with patient/system, irritation, compassion, frustration.

4 Management options. Do nothing, agitate, suggest private referral, referral to another consultant/hospital.

5 Wider issues. Length of waiting-lists, preferential treatment for fund-holders, role of general practitioner in political issues, should practice change its fundholding status and factors influencing the decision.

13.8

Mrs Falconer, a 30-year-old teacher, consults you saying that she is tired all the time. She is a new patient to your practice. She tells you that her previous doctor thought that she had ME and that she requires renewal of her long-term certification. On examination you cannot detect any physical abnormalities. She tells you that she has been fully investigated in the past but nothing has been found to be wrong. What factors would be relevant in this consultation?

CONSTRUCTS

1 Doctor's feelings. Feelings about the term ME, uncertainty about the diagnosis, heart-sink patient, establishment of doctor–patient relationship, dilemmas of sanctioning long-term certification. ? Support of previous doctor's diagnosis.

2 Patient expectations/beliefs. Understanding of ME, adoption of sick role, secondary gain, expectations of recovery/cure, psychological contributors, contextual issues.

3 Establishment of diagnosis. Review of history, work history, enquiry re family conflict, psychological assessment. ? Depression, reinvestigation, e.g. TFTs, FBC, virology, muscle biopsy.

4 Management. Certification issues, referral within and outside the practice, support, rehabilitation, antidepressants, alternative therapies.

13.9

Mr Barnes, a 35-year-old university lecturer, normally consults your senior partner who is currently on holiday. Your receptionist asks you what she should do about his request for a prescription for amoxycillin, which he says your partner always gives him when he has a cold. He is too busy to come to surgery and says that your partner never asks to see him when he requests such a prescription. He has no relevant past medical history. What issues are raised by this request?

CONSTRUCTS

1 Issues which need resolving with patient. Patient's expectations, mixed messages from partners, threat to autonomy, inconvenience.

2 Issues which need resolving with partner. Policy on issuing prescriptions, long-term relationships, threat to autonomy, prescribing policy.

3 Dilemmas for doctor. Duty to partner, duty to patient, 'good medicine', threat to doctor–patient relationships, threat to relationship with partner, implications of chosen action, to discuss or not, presenting united front to receptionist/patient.

4 Partnership issues. Practice policies, personal/shared lists, appropriate forum for discussion, practice formulary.

13.10

Mrs Craig, the niece of an 80-year-old patient of yours, who is suffering with mild dementia, comes to surgery to discuss her aunt's future care. She says she is not looking after herself properly but adamantly refuses to leave her own home. What issues might you wish to consider in this consultation?

CONSTRUCTS

1 Who is the patient? Mrs Craig, her aunt, other members of the family.

2 Options for the doctor. Do nothing, refer to social services, other members of PHCT, home care services, visit, arrange attendance allowance, negotiate with aunt.

3 Problems of absent patient. Ethical issues, confidentiality.

4 Patient autonomy. Issues of acting when uninvited, use of Mental Health Act, including Section 49, doctor–patient relationships.

Commentary 13

The surgery has a range of problems, in addition to some management issues in general practice. These range from homoeopathic treatment to HRT, first-aid kits, on-call work, ME and the use of antibiotics. The constructs include respect for patients' needs, doctor's feelings, patients' insistence on treatment, assessment of need, doctor's role, issues which need resolving with patient, issues which need resolving with partner and problems of absent patient.

MEQ 14

Assume you are in a suburban, five-partner practice which has a full complement of ancillary staff and is non-fundholding.

14.1

Mrs Norman is a 32-year-old married woman who came to see you last week complaining of a 3-week history of lower abdominal pain and vaginal discharge. Clinical examination suggested a diagnosis of pelvic inflammatory disease and the tests you performed are positive for gonorrhoea and *Chlamydia*. She returns today for the results of the tests. What would be your aims for this consultation?

CONSTRUCTS

1 Breaking bad news. Discussion of process, awareness of feelings – anger, denial, guilt,

2 Confidentiality. Inside and outside practice, husband, other sexual partners.

3 Implications for patient. Fertility, marriage, treatment, stigma of STD and referral to clinic.

4 Management. Adequate and appropriate, compliance, contact tracing, treatment of sexual partners, referral and its implications, follow-up – long- and short-term.

5 Social issues. Backup at home and within community.

14.2

Jean (28) has been trying to get pregnant since she married Brian (30) 3 years ago. Both are fit and well. As a preliminary investigation, you have arranged a sperm test for Brian. This shows a very low viable sperm count. The couple have returned today for the result. What would be your aims for this consultation?

CONSTRUCTS

1 Interpretation of husband's result. Explanation – low but not hopeless, need to repeat, adequacy of specimen, implications for further investigations/treatment, PMH.

2 Investigation of Jean. History, examination, preliminary blood tests, swabs, etc., menstrual and sexual history, temperature charts with explanation.

3 Relationships. Strain on marriage, guilt, blame, failure, whose problem, hopes, fears, expectations.

4 Doctor's role. Open approach, appropriate referral and investigation, provision of support, provide expectations, monitoring and prescription of expensive drugs.

14.3

Joan Dawkins, a 15-year-old, comes with her mother complaining that she is tired all the time. You cannot detect any physical abnormality and she denies any worries. After Joan leaves, Mrs Dawkins returns to tell you in confidence that Joan has missed her last two periods. She is worried that she may be pregnant. What issues does this consultation raise?

CONSTRUCTS

1 Causes of tiredness and amenorrhoea. Stress, hypothyroidism, other endocrine abnormalities, anorexia nervosa, pregnancy, depression, idiopathic.

2 Mother/daughter relationship. Encourage better communication – emphasis on process, empathy, open style, non-judgemental, relationship to other family members.

3 Ownership of problems. Mention of mother, Joan, boyfriend, doctor, other family members.

4 Doctor's role. Building relationship with Joan and mother, ensuring confidentiality, facilitation of family communication, investigations – pregnancy test, FBC, TFT, sugar.

5 Involvement of other agencies. Other members of PHCT, counsellors, psychologist, family therapist, gynaecologist.

6 Management issues. An agreed plan taking above into account.

14.4

George Westlake, a 55-year-old builder, is a diabetic. He was diagnosed 5 years ago and has always had blood sugars of 12–15 mmol/litre. He tells you that he has stopped taking his 5 mg glibenclamide tablets because he feels better without them. What issues does this raise and how can they be resolved?

CONSTRUCTS

1 Patient autonomy. Balance between patient autonomy and doctor control, informed consent, doctor paternalism/authoritarianism.

2 Medical problems. Risks, complications, retinopathy, neuropathy, cardiovascular problems, hypoglycaemic attacks.

3 Patient beliefs. Understanding of illness/test results, exploration (including process), mental state, awareness of complications, stigma of the illness, understanding of medication and diet.

4 Resolution. Understanding of patient's agenda, compromise, negotiation, involvement of PHCT, involvement of outside sources, e.g. hospital, self-help groups, etc.

14.5

Rosemary is a fit 20-year-old who has been on the combined oral contraceptive pill for 3 months. When she attends for a routine pill check, she tells you that she has lost all interest in sex. How might you be able to help?

CONSTRUCTS

1 Establish empathy. Emphasis on process – open approach, allowing plenty of time, non-judgemental, reassurance.

2 Patient's ideas, concerns, expectations. Whose problem, ideas on morality, previous relationship problems, learned behaviour, e.g. from peers, mother, etc., fear of pregnancy, fear of side-effects of pill.

3 Importance of good information-gathering. Sexual history, psychosocial problems, relationship with boyfriend, family dynamics, depressive symptoms, gynaecological symptoms.

4 Investigation of cause. Clinical examination, psychological assessment, elimination of endocrine cause, exclusion of causal relationship to pill.

5 Management. Counselling, referral – counsellor, specialist in psychosexual problems, gynaecologist, within practice – partner, practice nurse, etc., involvement of boyfriend, treatment of any physical cause that may be found.

14.6

Florence Matthews, a 34-year-old waitress, consults you because she has aching legs. On examination, she has mild, bilateral, below-knee varicose veins. You cannot detect any other abnormality. She asks you to sign her off 'on the sick' until she has them treated at the hospital. You know that the waiting-list at the hospital is over 6 months. Describe your response to her request.

CONSTRUCTS

1 Exploration of health beliefs. Range mentioned, open questions, non-judgemental approach, reasons for request.

2 Exploration of health agenda. Implications of working with varicose veins, concerns re the condition, its complications and treatment, personal experiences, experiences of others. ? Work problems, adoption of sick role, secondary gain.

3 Doctor's dilemma. Consideration of doctor – patient relationship, duty to DSS, duty to employers, duty to patient, recognition of own feelings – anger, frustration with system. ? Patient's advocate.

4 Appropriate clinical management. Support stockings/tights, only stockings on FP1, injection – hospital or surgery and factors governing decision, referral, dilemma re certification, modification of work pattern.

5 Wider issues. Symptom presented as ticket, exploration of other psychological morbidity – anxiety, depression, family problems, other contextual issues.

14.7

Wilhelmina Lloyd, a 50-year-old shop assistant, had a hysterectomy 3 months ago. She consults you for the seventh time this month with vague symptoms of malaise. You have fully examined and investigated her but cannot find any cause for her symptoms. What are the possible causes for her behaviour pattern and what can you do to help her?

CONSTRUCTS

1 Patient's unmet need. Undiagnosed physical illness, operation complications, menopausal symptoms, psychiatric illness, e.g. depression, alcoholism, concerns re hysterectomy, e.g. long-term complications, loss of femininity, etc.

2 Doctor's consulting behaviour. Collusion, ways of handling uncertainty, actions determined by feelings of frustration, anger or inadequacy.

3 Doctor's problems. Personal problems, practice dynamics, practice disharmony, burn-out, depression, inability to cope with difficult patients.

4 Patient behaviour. Patient's agenda, dependency, loneliness, ticket to another problem.

5 Solutions. Joint exploration, shared understanding, range of options discussed, confrontation, contracting, sharing of responsibility with other members of PHCT, psychologist, gynaecologist, etc.

14.8

Mary Walsh brings her 10-month-old son, Bertram, to see you as an emergency at the end of morning surgery. She tells you that he has been wheezing all night and ask whether this is asthma and if he should be admitted to hospital. What factors would you rely on to determine whether or not Bertram should be admitted to hospital?

CONSTRUCTS

1 History. Previous admissions, previous response to therapy, other medical history, e.g. cardiac problems, family history, duration and severity of attack and response to treatment.

2 Examination. General condition, colour, exhaustion, pulse, chest signs – silent chest, paradox, rhonchi/creps, anxiety of mother and child.

3 Environmental factors. Mother's coping ability, family dynamics, home circumstances, accessibility to hospital and practice, family wishes.

4 Mother's understanding and beliefs. Understanding of and familiarity with asthma, previous experiences.

5 Definition of problem. Certainty of diagnosis of asthma, consideration of other causes of wheeze, e.g. bronchiolitis, aspiration of foreign body, infection, appropriateness of mother's anxiety, mother's mental state.

6 Management plan. Agree with mother, taking above into account.

14.9

You discover that the number of house calls you are doing has increased dramatically lately. What might this be?

CONSTRUCTS

1 Your method of work. Increased recall rate, popularity, consulting style, stress, personal organization, practice organization, practice dynamics.

2 Patient demand. Increased list, poor patient education, altered demography of practice, increased expectations, unemployment, reduction in public transport services, epidemic.

3 Practice staff. Training, support, new staff, uncertainty.

4 Partners. Attitudes, commitment, holidays, sickness, consulting hours, attitudes to house calls.

5 Practice organization. Reduced availability, reduced accessibility, influence of patient participation groups.

14.10

Your senior partner asks you to consider a letter she has had from a local girls' boarding-school asking her to be their medical officer. She is keen to accept. What issues would you need to discuss in relation to this topic?

CONSTRUCTS

1 The school. Number of pupils, support staff, expectations of medical officer – on call, medical exams, staff care. Demands on time.

2 The practice perspective. Workload, implications for other patients, financial benefits – for partner or whole practice, other advantages to practice, private or NHS contract, prescribing, practice autonomy, individual or practice appointment, holiday/sickness arrangements.

3 Pupils. Ages, parental autonomy, availability of medical information, involvement in dangerous sports, etc.

4 Potential conflict. Parents, staff, pupils, other partners.

5 Partner. Why so keen to take up appointment – bored, afraid of burn-out, wish to increase income, flattered by offer, particular interest in this field.

Commentary 14

This surgery has a number of psychosexual problems and a number of problems related to pregnancy. The psychosexual problems are related to a low sperm count and lack of interest in sex. In addition there are a number of management problems related to becoming the medical officer and a problem related to the number of house calls being carried out by the practice. The constructs include breaking bad news, relationships, ownership of problem, patient beliefs, importance of good information-gathering, explanation of health beliefs, doctor's problem and environmental factors.

MEQ 15

The first patient in surgery is a 16-year-old boy, Stuart Gray, who has a 48-hour history of a sore throat and unremarkable findings on examination. Discuss your options for concluding this consultation.

CONSTRUCTS

1 Reassure. This is likely to be a viral infection and no action necessary.

2 Investigate. A full blood-count monospot to check for infectious mononucleosis is worth considering in this age-group.

3 Symptomatic treatment. Aspirin or paracetamol is likely to be adequate for this problem.

4 Antibiotic therapy. This has been shown to shorten the duration of severity of the illness very slightly.

5 Reason for attendance. Examples such as family pressure or anxiety.

6 Health promotion. Opportunity might be taken to move on to the area of STDs, accidents, and to cover topics such as smoking and use of drugs.

15.2

The next patient is a 46-year-old self-employed builder, John Collins, who was admitted to hospital 1 month ago with his first seizure. (Investigations at hospital since then have revealed no abnormalities but he has come to you to discuss his management.) How do you deal with important issues?

CONSTRUCTS

1 Drug therapy. Monotherapy is preferred. It should be optimized and continued until not less than 2 years have passed since last seizure.

2 Monitoring. Blood levels should be checked in the event of poor control.

3 Employment. The patient should avoid hazardous occupations, such as working machinery.

4 Driving. Should be seizure-free or only seizures during sleep for not less than 2 years.

5 Genetic risk. This should be discussed if there is a slight increase compared with the normal population.

15.3

The next patient, Sandra Miller, is a 74-year-old woman who complains of a 3–6 month history of difficulty sleeping. What are the possible underlying causes?

CONSTRUCTS

1 Physiological age. Should be considered.

2 Physical problems. Problems such as pains should be mentioned.

3 Psychological problems. For example, age anxiety or depression.

4 Psychiatric problems. For example, paraphrenia should be considered.

5 Pharmacological. For example, diuretics, β_2 agonists, caffeine.

15.4

A 6-year-old boy, David Kyle, is brought in by his parents. They found him playing with needles and syringes in a park. What are the immediate issues to be confronted?

CONSTRUCTS

1 Trauma. Puncture wounds – particularly ocular or entering an internal organ such as the pleural cavity – should be checked for.

2 Parental anxiety. This is likely to be high and should be mentioned.

3 Local sepsis. A dressing may be required, as may an antibiotic.

4 Hepatitis B. Immunoglobulin should be given and then he should be vaccinated.

5 HIV. There should be counselling, with possibly an immediate test organized and then repeated after 3 months.

15.5

The next patient is a 15-month-old girl, Angela Wilson, whose height and weight are below the third centile. On reviewing the notes it seems the child was normal at birth. Her failure to thrive has been worsening over the past 6 months. What features of the child's history would help you to define the cause?

CONSTRUCTS

1 Organic problems. GI, renal, metabolic or nutritional.

2 Non-organic problems. For example, psychological or social problems in the family.

3 Non-verbal communication. Observation of the parents' interaction with the child might reveal underlying tensions.

15.6

You start to sign the repeat prescriptions after surgery. What are the criteria by which you would judge the adequacy of a repeat prescribing system?

CONSTRUCTS

1 Prompt. Patients should be able to obtain a prescription within 24 hours of asking for it.

2 Accurate. Patients should get the prescription which the doctor has ordered.

3 A clear recall system. Receptionists, doctors and patients should know for how long the drug is to be prescribed and what will happen when that is exceeded.

4 Auditable. Information within the system should be able to be rapidly checked for under- or overprescribing.

15.7

While you are signing the repeat prescriptions, the mother of the 16-year-old boy in case 15.1 phones to ask why you did not give him the antibiotic which he normally gets. What issues does this raise?

CONSTRUCTS

1 Access. When do patients have access to doctors? What are the advantages and disadvantages of rapid phone access?

2 Patient expectations. They are obviously not being met for the mother, but is she the patient?

3 Evidence-based practice. Doctors' actions should be based on the best scientific evidence, or, if not, the reasons should be clear and justifiable.

4 Dealing with anger. Show awareness of the problems of this kind of consultation and have a well-worked-out strategy for defusing anger.

15.8

You next visit a 68-year-old man, James Black, at home: he is dying of lung cancer. What areas of care do you wish to address at such a preplanned terminal-care visit?

CONSTRUCTS

1 Bladder. Specifically check to see if there is any trouble with incontinence or retention of urine.

2 Bowels. Specific questions about diarrhoea, constipation, bedsores. An examination should be made for pressure points.

3 Mouth care. An examination of the mouth should be proposed.

4 Mobility. This should be encouraged. Morale, patient ideas, concerns and expectations should be dealt with in a positive light.

15.9

At the evening practice meeting you discuss the Royal College of General Practitioners Diabetes Guidelines Pack and you are asked to prepare a protocol from this. How do you proceed?

CONSTRUCTS

1 Identifying stakeholders. The receptionist, practice manager, district nurse and any other doctor in the practice interested in diabetic care should be mentioned.

2 Barriers to change. They should be identified and addressed.

3 Organization. The current organization of the practice will have to be reviewed to see whether it is adequate to cope with any problems.

4 Skills. Specific skills which are missing from within the practice. Those who will be responsible for organizing care for these patients should be identified and any lack of skill remedied.

5 Attitudes. These should be considered as a potential barrier and methods of motivation should be considered.

15.10

You decide to carry out an audit of satisfaction with the services your practice offers. Which dimensions should you study?

CONSTRUCTS

1 General satisfaction. A global estimate of patient satisfaction with the practice should be considered.

2 Access. Patients should be able to get to the practice easily and into the building once they do arrive there.

3 Availability. Consideration should be given to the time patients have to wait to be seen and how long they must wait once they reach the surgery.

4 Time. Patients' perception of the adequacy of the time allowed by the doctor or practice nurse should be considered.

5 Continuity. Patients should be able to see the same doctor each time as often as possible.

6 Premises. Are patients satisfied with the practice building and facilities, e.g. can they be overheard at the reception desk for the results of a pregnancy test?

Commentary 15

The surgery has a number of the 'bread-and-butter' problems of general practice, e.g. sore throat and sleeping difficulties, but in addition deals with some of the more difficult areas of guidelines and audit of satisfaction. The constructs include reason for attendance, genetic risk, employment, parental anxiety, non-verbal communication, a clear recall system, auditable, evidence-based practice, dealing with anger, mobility, identifying stakeholders and barriers to change.

MEQ 16

When you arrive for morning surgery you find a 7-year-old, Alison Burke, with her father in the treatment room. She sustained a 5 cm laceration to her forehead the previous day. What are the implications of this presentation?

CONSTRUCTS

1 Head injury. This must be assessed for local and internal trauma.

2 Appropriate action taken in case of non-accidental injury. This should be considered by the candidate and specific steps taken to confirm or exclude this.

3 Referral to accident and emergency. This should be considered depending on the candidate's confidence and his/her ability to assess the problem in the practice.

4 Parental anxiety. This should be explicitly mentioned and addressed by the candidate.

16.2

Jane Smith, a 17-year-old girl, presents next requesting the morning-after pill. What are the important ethical and practice management aspects of this consultation *vis-à-vis* patient autonomy?

CONSTRUCTS

1 Patient autonomy. Extent to which the doctor acknowledges the problems of the direct request from a patient for a specific therapy.

2 Doctor's own feelings. Religious or moral objections to complying with the patient's request should be considered.

3 Availability of contraception. Preventability of the consultation: consider the practice's provision of contraceptives.

16.3

Alex Thomson comes in next, a 48-year-old man who has been thrown out of the flat he shares with two other men because of his disruptive behaviour most evenings, when intoxicated. How do you assess his problem and what help can you offer him?

CONSTRUCTS

1 Domestic situation. Should be explored.

2 Physical problems. Problems arising from alcohol abuse should be mentioned – in this case, specifically injuries and toxic confusional states.

3 Psychiatric problems. Depression or dementia should be considered.

4 Referral. Social work department for housing needs. Counselling agencies such as AA.

16.4

James Morton, your next patient, is a 74-year-old retired miner who was bereaved a year ago. He is currently experiencing back pain, headaches, constipation and insomnia. The main physical findings are the non-verbal cues, which suggest depressed mood. What difficulties might you experience in communicating a diagnosis of depression to this patient?

CONSTRUCTS

1 Health beliefs. He may consider an underlying physical cause to be his problem.

2 Sensory impairment. He may have hearing loss from the previous occupation.

3 Cultural gap. Depending on age and background the doctor may have difficulty conveying message to the patient.

4 Social issues. Opinions of friends and neighbours re condition.

16.5

A 37-year-old married university lecturer, whose family you know very well, comes requesting the OCP. Her husband had a vasectomy 2 years ago, after the birth of their third child. What are the implications of this request?

CONSTRUCTS

1 Awareness of patient's hidden agenda. Since the doctor is a family friend, the patient may wish to enlist his/her support.

2 Awareness of doctor's own feelings and motivations. These should be acknowledged and difficulty with dealing with them stated.

3 Preventive interventions. The implications of avoiding STDs should be considered if a new partner is involved.

16.6

Dennis McDaid, a 27-year-old temporary resident, is next. He requests a prescription for oral methadone. What are the implications of this?

CONSTRUCTS

1 Withdrawal. Failure to prescribe may lead to severe withdrawal symptoms.

2 Risk reduction. Full exploration of the patient's lifestyle and pattern of drug use with a view to minimizing risks.

3 Practice policies. Prescribing or failing to prescribe in accordance with laid-down practice policies.

4 Notification. Is the patient a notified drug addict and, if not, is the Home Office to be involved?

16.7

Ann Stewart is a 27-year-old personal secretary who has just discovered she is pregnant. She asks you about the precautions she should take before going on holiday to Kenya for 6 weeks. What is your response?

CONSTRUCTS

1 Antimalarials. Yes, probably chloroquine or proguanil. Avoiding dihydrofolate reductase inhibitors, e.g. pyrimethamine, mefloquine.

2 Vaccinations. Avoiding live vaccines, polio, yellow fever.

3 General advice. Exposure to infectious diseases, including STDs. Excessive heat and sun.

4 Other sources of information. If uncertain, the candidate should turn to sources of reference, either in the practice or remote.

5 Advisability of travel. Should she go?

16.8

A 46-year-old man, John Smith, then visits complaining of impotence. He says he wants to take the pills your partner gave him 20 years ago for the same thing. How might you be able to help?

CONSTRUCTS

1 Physical causes. Exclude problems such as diabetes, vascular insufficiency.

2 Psychological problems. Recent traumas.

3 Social. Change of partner, stress, change of location.

4 Management plan. Agree with him investigations and plan of management.

16.9

John Brown, a 46-year-old businessman, comes in requesting a sickness certificate because of increasing business pressure due to debt. He reminds you that he had a 'possible MI' 3 years ago. How do you respond and what implications might this have for your future relationship with the patient?

CONSTRUCTS

1 Awareness of patient's hidden agenda. Wish to evade responsibilities or manipulate doctor.

2 Responsibility to society. Unless genuine illness is present, a certificate may not be given in good faith.

3 Problem with future relationship. The candidate should be well aware that actions in this consultation and the particular decision on whether or not to supply the requested certificate will have an effect on the future relationship with this patient.

16.10

Alan James is a 33-year-old electrical engineer with a non-specific chest pain today for the first time. He has no risk factors for IHD. What can you do to minimize the possibility of somatic fixation?

CONSTRUCTS

1 Clinical competence. Good history and examination go a long way to minimize patient's fears.

2 Exploration. Patient's ideas, concerns and expections. In particular, this may lead to insight into recent or remote family event which would lead him to conclude that he is more susceptible.

3 Strong reassurance. Should be given if at all possible.

4 Patient's viewpoint. Recognize the patient's point of view with regard to the question of referral and address reason for non-referral.

Commentary 16

This surgery contains a number of problems which have a social overtone, e.g. the morning-after pill, thrown out of flat, request for the pill when husband has had vasectomy and prevention for a pregnant patient who is travelling to Kenya. The constructs include parental anxiety, doctor's own feelings, domestic situation, cultural gap, awareness of patient's hidden agenda, risk reduction, notification, advisability of travel, responsibility to society and exploration.

MEQ 17

You are one of six partners in a group practice working from a purpose-built surgery. The partnership operates a personal list system whenever possible and has a 10-minute appointment system.

17.1

Your first patient is Tracy Bell, aged 21. She works at the checkout counter in a local food supermarket. Tracy tells you that she has read in a woman's magazine about 'Norplant' and asks if you could provide her with this means of contraception. What information should be provided for Tracy and how might a decision about this treatment be achieved?

CONSTRUCTS

1 Doctor's feelings. Is candidate accepting of this presentation (quote from magazine) and does he/she use the information in a positive way?

2 Patient's reason for request. How well does candidate explore reasons?

3 Doctor's response. Does candidate fully consider contraception options?

4 Doctor's knowledge. Is candidate fully aware of possible limited knowledge?

5 Medicolegal. Are medicolegal implications adequately considered?

6 Decision process. Does candidate demonstrate rational thought in reaching a decision?

7 Anticipatory care. Does candidate take the opportunity of discussing cervical smears, safer sex, STDs, etc.?

17.2

Having just completed the consultation with Tracy Bell, you are interrupted by a phone call from a local hotel. Apparently a visitor from North America, Mr Canyon, aged 64, has requested an urgent visit on account of the very recent onset of severe chest pain. Outline your likely strategy for dealing with such a situation (excluding the acute clinical assessment and management of his chest pain).

CONSTRUCTS

1 Doctor's response. Does candidate emphasize the importance of content of initial telephone response?

2 Action plan. Is candidate aware of importance of 'thinking through' a plan of action?

3 Action plan details. Is a logical and clinically sound plan devised?

4 Implications for practice. Are attempts made to reduce disruption for waiting patients and the practice in general?

5 Effect on family. Are relatives and/or friends considered?

6 Getting patient home. Is flying (after possible MI) considered?

17.3

You return to your surgery 1 hour later. Your patients have all rebooked at a later time, extending the length of your surgery. The next patient is a woman aged 50, who is a lawyer and the wife of a company director. She has come for a BP check and to renew her prescription for atenolol and temazepam. She enters your room in a fury, saying, 'This service is despicable; I thought there was a Patient's Charter.' How would you respond?

CONSTRUCTS

1 Effect of waiting. Is candidate empathetic concerning anxiety worsened by long wait?

2 Patient concerns. Does candidate fully explore and consider possible hidden agenda in addition to presenting problems?

3 Coping with stress. Are communication skills demonstrated in defusing stress?

4 Future consultations. Does candidate demonstrate awareness of importance of a satisfactory consultation for future relationships?

5 Is treatment appropriate? Does candidate demonstrate the skills necessary to provide good clinical management?

17.4

Your next patient, Mr Cyril Rollington, has just joined your practice. He informs you that he has recently been appointed as charge nurse in your local district general hospital. He tells you that he is HIV-positive but requests that the information be kept entirely confidential between you and him. What dilemmas does this present and how may they be resolved?

CONSTRUCTS

1 Needs of patient. Does candidate fully explore reasons for request?

2 Doctor's response. Is candidate fully aware of sensitive nature of response? Does candidate discuss fully the issue of confidentiality?

3 Implications for others. Are these comprehensively addressed?

4 Other agencies. Is candidate aware of and willing to consult other agencies?

17.5

Your next patient is a 35-year-old married woman, Mrs Sandra Simpkins. She tells you that, despite trying to conceive for some 12 months, she has not yet become pregnant and asks if there is anything that should be done at this stage. (a) List the items of information you need to know before you answer her question. (b) What explanation would you give her about general management of failure to conceive?

CONSTRUCTS

1 **Attitudes.** Does candidate explore attitude of patient and husband?

2 **Autonomy.** Is there full exploration of patient's ideas and expectations?

3 **Clinical competence.** Does candidate exhibit clinical competence in the range of gynaecological, sexual and medical areas explored?

4 **Communication.** Does candidate display communication skills? Is content of communication appropriate?

17.6

Susan Springwell, aged 48, is terminally ill with carcinomatosis secondary to ovarian carcinoma. She is cared for by her husband Jack and an unmarried daughter Clare, aged 22. The district nurse speaks to you prior to a routine house visit, stating that, despite oral diamorphine, Mrs Springwell is in severe pain and extremely distressed. How can you help?

CONSTRUCTS

1 **Concerns of nurse.** Are these adequately appreciated and addressed?

2 **Needs of carers.** Physical needs considered? Emotional needs considered?

3 Clinical competence. Does candidate display clinical competence?

4 Other agencies. Are they recognized and considered?

5 Management issues. Has the candidate prepared an action plan?

17.7

John Brown, a single, 25-year-old, truck-driver, consults you. He tells you that 2 years ago, while driving a large vehicle, he knocked down a cyclist, who subsequently died. He has recently had difficulty sleeping and has been unable to work for the past 2 weeks, saying that he is too fearful to drive to work. How can you help?

CONSTRUCTS

1 Listening to patient. Does candidate attach sufficient importance to this?

2 Empathy. Does candidate imply empathetic support?

3 Accident details. Does candidate enquire about details?

4 Death of cyclist. Are implications discussed?

5 Current symptoms. Is comprehensive and appropriate psychiatric history taken?

6 Support network. Is current support network explored? Is future support network addressed?

7 Management. Is an appropriate management plan developed?

17.8

The senior partner of the practice is on holiday and you have been allocated a patient from his chronic visiting list. Mrs Cecilia Drummond-Smith is a wealthy widow aged 78, living in a large house. On arrival your first observation is that she seems to be extremely fit and well. From her sparsely written medical records you note that she had a 'funny turn' some 2 years previously but there have been no medical events since then and she is not on any medication. She greets you warmly and immediately pours you a glass of sherry. Outline your management of this situation.

CONSTRUCTS

1 Doctor's feelings. Does candidate acknowledge likely feelings?

2 Patient's needs. Does the candidate attempt to identify her needs?

3 Maintaining relationship. Is candidate aware of the need to, and prepared to make an effort to, establish a good relationship?

4 Rationing of care. Does the candidate address the importance of resources?

5 Process of informing. Does the candidate sensitively manage the process of informing patient's own general practitioner of the dilemma surrounding the visit?

6 Effect of informing. Is candidate sensitive to effect on his partner of the management discussion.

17.9

After a busy day in the practice you are off duty and awakened at 2.00 a.m. by a telephone call. An acquaintance informs you that his son, aged 4, is desperately ill with an asthma attack and requests that you come at once. Outline the problems presented by this situation and how they may be resolved.

CONSTRUCTS

1 Doctor's feelings. Are these fully acknowledged and discussed?

2 Doctor's concerns. Are they identified (e.g. alcohol, equipment, etc)?

3 Doctor's response. Is this positive and appropriate for an emergency situation?

4 Action. Is action plan adequate to meet emergency need?

5 Parental motives. Are possible motives identified?

6 Education. Is sensitive and appropriate education planned?

17.10

You are asked by the headmaster of a local comprehensive school to provide an afternoon of sexual health education to a mixed class of sixth-form boys and girls. Outline your proposed structure and content.

CONSTRUCTS

1 Doctor's enthusiasm. Is this recognized as an excellent opportunity?

2 Doctor's concerns. Are concerns such as lack of knowledge addressed?

3 Planning and information-gathering. Are plans logical and appropriate?

4 Pupils' needs. Are they correctly identified?

5 Effect on pupils and staff. Is candidate aware of diversity of effect?

Commentary 17

The surgery deals with some of the common general practice problems, e.g. difficulty sleeping and funny turn, and also some of the newer practice concepts of Norplant and Patient's Charter. The constructs used include anticipatory care, getting home, effect of waiting, autonomy, concerns of nurse, support network, rationing of care, process of informing, parental motives and effect of sex education on pupils and staff.

MEQ 18

18.1

Your first patient on a Monday morning is Sarah Simpson, aged 17. She requests the morning-after pill. You see from her records that there have been three similar requests over the past few months. How would you respond?

CONSTRUCTS

1 Doctor's feelings. Does the candidate recognize likely feelings: first patient on Monday. ? Religious objections.

2 Patient autonomy. Does candidate recognize and accept that patient should be involved in decision-making process?

3 Communication skills. Is there evidence of good communication skills?

4 Contraceptive problems. Does candidate demonstrate understanding of how this repeated problem may have arisen?

5 Agreed plan. Is a sound plan for current situation and the future agreed?

18.2

Mrs Robertson, aged 51, is your next patient. She has come at the behest of her husband as he feels she should have HRT, but she is not particularly keen. How can you help?

CONSTRUCTS

1 Husband's agenda. Does candidate recognize that husband may

197

have special reasons? Are possible reasons adequately identified?

2 Mrs Robertson's feelings. Are these fully explored?

3 Mrs Robertson's knowledge. Does candidate attempt to find out level of knowledge and understanding?

4 Information-sharing. Does candidate recognize the importance of information-sharing?

5 Empathy. Is doctor empathetic with Mrs Robertson's conflict and dilemma?

6 Clinical knowledge. Does candidate provide evidence that he has sound clinical knowledge in this area of medicine?

7 Reaching decision. Is there evidence of a logical approach to decision-making?

18.3

Your next patients are a couple who are about to proceed on their honeymoon to Kenya some 3 weeks hence. They say they have had all the appropriate vaccinations but request prescriptions for antimalarials. How do you respond?

CONSTRUCTS

1 Communication. Does candidate demonstrate good communication skills and attempt to 'share' in their excitement and expectations?

2 Couple's knowledge. Does candidate assess this?

3 Physical protection. Does candidate strongly emphasize how important this is and identify means of achieving it?

4 Process of decision. Does candidate clearly know how to make a decision on choice of antimalarial?

5 Compliance. Does candidate recognize the importance of clear explanation concerning compliance?

7 Clinical safety. Does the candidate provide safe clinical advice, remembering possible pregnancy, drug interactions, etc.?

18.4

In the middle of your morning surgery you receive a call from the mother of a 3-year-old child. She informs you that Billy has had diarrhoea for 2 days and is crying with abdominal pain. You decide to visit in 1 hour on completion of your morning surgery. When you arrive at the house you are informed by a neighbour that the mother dialled 999 and that the child is now on the way to hospital. What are the implications of this event?

CONSTRUCTS

1 Doctor's feelings. Does candidate recognize likely feelings?

2 Doctor's stress. Is there recognition that stress must be 'contained' and managed?

3 Needs of the patient. Is there acknowledgement that despite doctor's stress the needs of the patient are of prime concern?

4 Implications. Is there recognition of the implications of mother's actions, including cost?

5 Resolution. Does the candidate develop an acceptable plan?

18.5

Later that day you visit a patient living in the same street as Billy. The patient says, 'All the neighbours are furious because you refused to visit Billy.' (Billy was discharged without treatment following the emergency 999 call.) What do you do?

CONSTRUCTS

1 Personal control. Is there emphasis on the importance of controlling anger?

2 Empathy for 'panic'. Does the candidate recognize that the action was probably on account of panic?

3 Information-gathering. Does the candidate appreciate the value of calmly collecting information from different sources before discussion with parents?

4 Communication with parents. Does the candidate stress the importance of a non-confrontational approach to parents?

5 Medicolegal implications. Is the candidate aware of importance of accurate contemporaneous note-keeping?

18.6

In surgery your next patient is Susan, a 15-year-old girl with Down's syndrome. She is accompanied by the officer-in-charge of the residential home where she lives. You are informed that Susan has been very sexually provocative and there is concern that she might become pregnant. It is requested that you arrange contraception in the form of Depo-provera by injection. How would you respond?

CONSTRUCTS

1 Respect. Is candidate willing to respect autonomy of the mentally disabled?

2 Risk assessment. Does candidate enquire into risk assessment and current prevention procedures?

3 Consequence of pregnancy. Does candidate fully appreciate the extensive implications of pregnancy in this situation?

4 Interested parties. Are other parties taken into consideration, e.g. parents, other residents, staff?

5 Agreed plan. Is this developed in an ethical and appropriate manner?

18.7

Your next patient is a 36-year-old woman. She has three children aged 5, 7 and 11 and is recently divorced. She informs you that she was sterilized after the third pregnancy. She is now living with a man aged 24 and they wish to have a child. She asks that you refer her for reversal of sterilization. What are the issues involved in such a request?

CONSTRUCTS

1 Time. Is there an appreciation that considerable time for discussion in a non-judgemental manner will be required?

2 Hidden agenda. Is there full appreciation of a possible hidden agenda and has the candidate speculated on what this might be?

3 Needs of partner. Is there recognition of and sympathy for the possible needs of her partner?

4 Procedure difficulties. Is there an understanding that the technical method employed for sterilization will affect outcome of reversal procedure?

5 Resolution. Is rational plan developed? Are other options discussed?

18.8

Present out-of-hours arrangements in your practice are that the duties are shared equally between all partners. You learn that a national deputizing service is offering its service to your practice and the youngest partner in the practice has, at the weekly practice meeting, asked that he be allowed to use this service. What are the implications of this request?

CONSTRUCTS

1 Patients' needs. Are these fully recognized as being of prime importance?

2 Partner's needs. Is the candidate fully aware of possible problems in the personal life of the youngest partner, e.g. marriage, small children, health, elderly parents, etc.?

3 Colleagues' feelings. Awareness of colleagues' feelings and suggestions for resolution.

4 Cost implications. Have implications for all concerned been identified?

5 Managing change. Has a satisfactory plan been developed?

6 Interested parties. Is it recognized that other parties (e.g. FHSA/health board) will have an interest?

18.9

Your next patient is a 9-year-old girl, Patricia. Her mother has brought her to see you following a recent hospital admission when it was diagnosed that Patricia has diabetes. Speculate on the future events in the life of Patricia.

CONSTRUCTS

1 Patient's understanding. Does candidate emphasize the importance of patient knowledge and education concerning diabetes?

2 Support network. Is current and future support network discussed?

3 Insight. Has candidate insight into possible rejection of diagnosis, poor compliance, teenage rebellion, etc.?

4 Predictive skills. Has candidate a catholic approach to the wide range of possible future problems?

18.10

Your practice receives a letter from the medical director of your FHSA/health board in which you are informed that prescriptions for drugs acting on the respiratory system for your practice cost 25% above the national average. What action should you take?

CONSTRUCTS

1 Doctor's feelings. Is candidate aware that a doctor may have very strong feelings regarding cost containment? May feel that budget should be 'open-ended' and according to need, as deemed by doctor. Action may be determined by such opinion.

2 Data collection. Does candidate approach data collection in a logical manner?

3 Practice demography. Does candidate make full use of demography and additional 'peculiar' features of practice in assessing response and planning action?

4 Audit. Is audit of respiratory system drugs conducted in realistic and potentially informative manner?

5 Action. Is a rational plan developed?

Commentary 18

This surgery dealt with some of the practical problems presented to a general practitioner, e.g. travel abroad, morning-after pill, furious neighbours, deputizing and prescription costs. The constructs include contraceptive problems, husband's agenda, clinical safety, doctor's stress, empathy for panic, interested parties, procedure difficulties, managing change, support network and practice demography.

MEQ 19

Mr Harry Hughes, aged 54, comes to see you in morning surgery. He has been on atenolol 50 mg a day for 2 years for control of his BP. His BP on treatment has been satisfactory. Today he throws his atenolol pills on the desk and declares that he is fed up with taking your pills; he is going to try homoeopathy. What factors should you consider in trying to resolve this situation?

CONSTRUCTS

1 Patient's agenda. Reasons for declaration, e.g. side-effects, health beliefs (family, media, friends), lack of faith in traditional medicine, conflict with general practitioner, Hospital, illness of friend, lack of understanding of hypertension as a risk factor.

2 Doctor's agenda. Feelings, irritation, upset, own ideas about alternative therapy, own ideas about importance of hypertension as a risk factor, loss of face/conflict with a patient, failing to establish satisfactory doctor–patient relationship.

3 Restoring/maintaining rapport. Ability to cope with this situation, listening to patient, exploring concerns, negotiating happy result, respecting patient autonomy, monitoring situation, allowing patient to return without fear of upset.

4 Management of hypertension. Importance of Mr Hughes's hypertension, initial readings, end-organ damage, alternative treatments (drug and non-drug), patients allowed to stop treatment under review – results, reference to literature. Associated risk factors, e.g. smoking, weight, cholesterol, stress, exercise, salt, family history, associated diseases, e.g. DM, IHD, etc.

19.2

Mrs Kay Kettering, a 52-year-old divorcee, attends to enquire about HRT. She tells you that she has read that it is good for one's sex life. What areas do you cover in this consultation?

CONSTRUCTS

1 Patient's agenda. ? New relationship, other reasons for HRT, e.g. osteoporosis, IHD, strokes, symptoms of menopause, knowledge of which symptoms will respond to treatment. Level of her reading about HRT.

2 Doctor's agenda. Attitude towards patient's request for more information, e.g. irritation, lack of knowledge, use of practice nurse, clinic, leaflets, videos, time-consuming consultation, opportunity for health promotion, own feelings about HRT.

3 Explanation of risks vs. benefits. Accurate information about acknowledged risk factors and benefits of HRT, mention of cost–benefits.

4 Patient management. Respecting autonomy, appropriate examination, use of time, i.e. to consider facts, to make informed decision, need for review, various methods available, length of time on HRT.

5 Reaching decision. Is there evidence of logical approach to decision-making?

19.3

Debbie Drake, aged 15, attends your surgery unaccompanied. She looks embarrassed, and asks if she can have the morning-after pill. Discuss your management.

CONSTRUCTS

1 Patient's feelings. Embarrassed, level of courage to attend, why unaccompanied, ability to communicate with parents, boyfriend, what actually happened, is it her first request, fear of pregnancy, STDs.

2 Doctor's agenda. Attitude to under-age sex, PCP, explanation of confidentiality issues, attitude to parents, attitude to teenage health issues, awareness of sensitivity of consultation, awareness of time management.

3 Obtaining accurate history. Timing of intercourse, actual risk of conception, appropriateness of PCP. ? Need for IUCD. ? Pregnant. Assessment for risk of STDs, safe sex, future contraception, window of opportunity.

4 Safety-netting. Explanation of PCP, risk of pregnancy, what happens if vomit/conceive anyway, future relationship with Debbie, relationship with Debbie's parents, need for review. Deregulating emergency contraception/Gillick/reference to literature.

19.4

Your next patient is Mr Reginald Wright, who complains of recent onset of rectal bleeding. On rectal examination you feel a hard mass that you are fairly sure is malignant. He has no obvious clinical spread. How do you handle this situation?

CONSTRUCTS

1 Rapport with patient. Establish relationship which makes it easier for patient to ask questions, feel as comfortable as possible, assess current need for information from patient, need for honesty if appropriate.

2 Explanation. What has been found in terms acceptable to patient, principles of breaking bad news, acknowledge own availability of time/access to further information, open-door approach.

3 Management. Management plan, urgent referral to hospital, choice of consultant, biopsy, possible surgery, involvement of team, e.g. Macmillan nurses, district nurses, visiting postoperatively.

4 Doctor's role. Your own feelings/distress at this situation, room for optimism, long-term management, importance of diagnosis and note-keeping, communication with relatives, appropriateness of confidentiality.

19.5

At coffee time your health visitor suggests that the practice should start a 'quit-smoking' group. How do you respond?

CONSTRUCTS

1 Health visitor's reasons for suggestion. Just been on course, real need, protecting job. What audience does he/she want to reach, e.g. mothers, teenagers, general public? How does he/she suggest doing this, posters, etc.? Effectiveness of method chosen.

2 Dealing with staff suggestions. Show appropriate interest, encourage more suggestions, appraise each one appropriately, forum for discussion, e.g. by practice meeting or practice manager. ? Prize for best suggestion.

3 Doctor/practice involvement. Timing, doctor/nurse involvement, space, skills for group leadership, cost, benefits, e.g. happy patients, results in patients actually giving up.

4 Appraisal of suggestion. Mechanism for practice making decisions, effectiveness of quit-smoking groups, other practices' experiences, literature, other methods available, e.g. opportunistic, leaflets, nicotine substitutes. Assessment of motivation of patients attending a group.

19.6

Your first visit is to a 35-year-old woman who is just home from hosptial, having had a complete miscarriage at 10 weeks' gestation in her first pregnancy. Your partner sent her in as an emergency two nights ago. What areas do you wish to cover on this visit?

CONSTRUCTS

1 Her experiences of medical care. Emergency doctor, doctors and nurses at hospital. What does she understand, what has she been told, what drugs, e.g. anti-D, has she been given?

2 Patient's feelings. Sense of loss, grieving, importance of pregnancy, guilt, need to blame someone, level of support, e.g. husband/family, her own health beliefs.

3 Physical condition. Bleeding, pain, temperature, need for further follow-up, midwife intervention, appropriateness of general practitioner visiting.

4 Explanation. Showing you care, explanations of health beliefs, misgivings, future pregnancies, risks involved, achieving a healthy pregnancy, contraception, Miscarriage Association.

19.7

You are contacted at 3.00 a.m. while on call for the practice by Mrs Shirley Collins. She wonders if you can pop out to see her 4-year-old daughter, Lucy, who has a temperature of 102°F. How do you respond?

CONSTRUCTS

1 Management of phone call. Accurate information-gathering, e.g. address, phone number, other symptomatology, management of patient so far, reasons for concern.

2 Doctor's feelings. Irritating request, irritating time, trying to survive on call, trying to avoid a complaint, trying to modify help-seeking behaviour vs. problems of not visiting when requested.

3 Doctor's assessment. Past knowledge of patient, balanced assessment of health risk to girl, ability to negotiate plan by telephone consultation and allow safety-netting, decision to visit if appropriate and why decision was made, effect on doctor if decides not to visit, night-visit fee.

19.8

Your PACT figures show that the practice is 30% above the FHSA average for respiratory drugs. Your fund manager suggests that you should make savings on these drugs. What areas do you cover in your discussion?

CONSTRUCTS

1 Reasons for high spending. More inhaled steroids prescribed, more expensive than B_2 agonists, recommendations in BTS guidelines, ? more asthmatics picked up in your practice indicating 'good practice', presence of asthma clinic, practice policy on expensive drugs, learning from drug reps, *BNF*, drugs and therapeutics bulletin, consultants, peers, hospital policy on asthma prescribing, high numbers of certain disease, e.g. CF. High use of cromoglycate, high use of new, more expensive steroids, few generic products prescribed, no practice formulary, formulary needs updating, ? deliberate overspending to massage budget, no review of repeat prescribing.

2 Ways of reducing spending, where appropriate. Formulary, look at methods of low prescribing in cheaper practices, PACT level 3, audit, educational meetings, literature searches, communication with hospital consultants, more generic prescribing, intensive review of repeat prescribing.

3 Ways of increasing prescribing. Identify more asthmatics (rule of halves, Tudor Hart), follow BTS guidelines strictly in all patients, improving asthma care, more use of modern delivery techniques, prescribing expensive drugs, cynical overprescribing, rebelling against government restrictions.

4 Other issues. Patient autonomy, right to choose own medication, doctor autonomy, right to prescribe what he/she wants, increasing management intervention in general practice, indicative prescribing budgets, implications of drug savings for practice, for government, for taxpayer, for nation.

19.9

Your full-time female partner proposes at a partnership meeting that she would like to introduce personal lists in the practice. What areas should be covered in the ensuing discussion?

CONSTRUCTS

1 Female partner. Why is she requesting this, what does she see as the benefit? Fewer female patients, more chance to practice family medicine, know patients better, less shopping around for opinions, less family planning, gynaecology, obstetrics, depression, anxiety, etc.

2 Other partners. More female patients, why should they change? Like things as they are, change is an effort, already feel stressed, how to allocate patients to doctors – by patient choice? by doctor choice? – previous experience of personal-list medicine, effect on trainees, locums, assistants, holidays, etc., mean that no such thing as true personal list, if seeing patient who would rather not see you then more chance for complaints.

3 Patients. What do they feel, does this matter, should you ballot them? Less choice of doctor to meet their requirement, less chance to get differing opinions, will feel that different doctors have separate expertise, their autonomy in choice of doctor, able to see other doctor on their general practitioner's half-day, etc.

4 Team. Having to make change, ? notify FHSA/health commissions, dealing with disgruntled patients. Do other members of team work personal lists, e.g. health visitors, district nurses, what do they feel, who will run clinics, e.g. child health surveillance, diabetes, asthma, well woman, is more training required for staff and doctors?

19.10

Your practice manager informs you that your ECG machine is beyond repair. It will cost £3000 to buy a new one. What would you expect to be discussed in the decision to replace it?

CONSTRUCTS

1 Is another one needed? If really beyond repair, is an ECG machine really necessary? Many would say no. Difficulty in maintenance, expertise in reading them, time required to perform them. Is nurse time better used on other things, e.g. income-generating, do we carry them on call, how close is local hospital, do they offer ECG services? This would be read by people with more expertise. Does a normal ECG reading influence your decision-making in a clinical diagnosis of MI.

2 Pro-ECG lobby. Useful in reassuring patients, demonstrating well-equipped surgery, keeps patient care in the surgery, less expense in referrals to hospital, how would hospital cope with increased workload if practice didn't have one, past experience in using ECG. How do patients feel if no longer have equipment they are used to? Danger of losing patients, increased general practitioner morale in providing better service.

3 Option to buy one. How to raise money, charities, patients' gifts, ? insurance, FHSA funding, own pocket. Audit use of ECG in past year: has it proved worthwhile, has it changed clinical decisions? Should you get one that reads ECGs as well, would you trust it? What could money be used on if not ECG, more patient benefit from alternative equipment?

Commentary 19

This deals with a wide-ranging surgery, with alternative medicine considered in addition to some problems of female patients with HRT and the morning-after pill. There is also some health promotion regarding smoking. The surgery also deals with management issues of PACT data and personal lists. The constructs include restoring and maintaining rapport, risks vs. benefits, safety-netting, dealing with staff suggestions, sense of loss, management of phone calls, reasons for high spending, female partner and the need for equipment.

MEQ 20

A 50-year-old businessman, Ray Hunter, attends your surgery complaining of difficulty sleeping and of lethargy. He attributes it all to regular business trips to America. He wonders if you could just prescribe him a few sleeping pills. How would you hope to handle this consultation?

CONSTRUCTS

1 Establish rapport. Demonstrate willingness to listen, concern, appropriate consulting style, looking for diagnostic clues in body language, speech, appearance, etc.

2 Establish accurate diagnosis. Explore patient's own ideas in full, may be just jet lag but consider stress, anxiety, depression (reference to defeat depression, importance of not missing diagnosis) and other conditions such as thyroid problems and anaemia.

3 Options to treat. Non-drug, counselling, helping sleep, e.g. advice about less alcohol, warm drink before bed, self-hypnosis, relaxation techniques, options of prescribing benzodiazepines and their real risk (reference to literature), treating depression if present and various methods used in this, need for follow-up.

4 Patient autonomy/Doctor's feelings. Patient's right to have treatment of choice if understands risks, vs. doctor's feelings about nature of request. Option of acceding to request quickly vs. exploring problem in full.

20.2

A 26-year-old secretary, Jill Hodges, comes to say that she has stopped taking the OCP because she and her husband wish to try for a child. She says that they want to do all the right things for a healthy pregnancy. What areas should be covered in the consultation?

CONSTRUCTS

1 Her health beliefs. ? Stopping pill for 3 months, pill must get out of the system, ideas about timing/method of conception, what is concerning her, ideas about safe foods, pets, maternal age, friends/ relatives with problems, etc.

2 Healthy pregnancy issues. Diet, safe and non-safe foods (list of foods and risks they engender), vitamins, folic acid, smoking, alcohol, infectious diseases, rubella antibodies, blood group.

3 Risk factors. Previous obstetric and gynaecological history. Any disasters, any problems with husband, any family history, is she known to have diabetes, hypertension, valvular disease, etc.?

20.3

Mrs Ellen Brown, a 42-year-old woman with frequent somatic symptoms, attends with a history of headaches for the past month. They appear to be tension headaches. She asks if she could pay for a private brain-scan; she is not insured. How would you hope to reach a satisfactory conclusion to this consultation?

CONSTRUCTS

1 Her agenda. What is frightening her this time, severity of symptoms, friends'/relatives' health, media scares, her right to purchase investigations.

2 Your agenda. How does this request make you feel? Not trusted, not clinically competent, previous errors with diagnosis in this patient, your confidence in diagnosis of tension headache. What if you are proved wrong? 'Patients know best', availability of resources, gatekeeper role, maintaining doctor–patient relationship.

3 Ethical issues. What is fair, should she pay, should NHS pay? Her autonomy to have test, the net good versus harm of acceding to/refusing her request. Where will demands end with this patient?

20.4

You are in surgery when the receptionist interrupts your consultation with an urgent visit request. Mrs Brown is on the telephone worried about her 58-year-old husband, who has a history of angina; she asks if you could 'come quickly doctor, I'm sure he's having a heart attack'. What do you do?

CONSTRUCTS

1 Handling telephone consultation. Obtaining accurate information, name, address, phone number, history, severity of illness, immediate care, e.g. recovery position if unconscious, dial 999, exude calm and caring, promise visit.

2 Actions at surgery. Conclude current consultation with explanation, inform receptionists, patients in waiting-room, etc., collect equipment from surgery if necessary, e.g. ECG, emergency bag, i.v. equipment.

3 At house. History and examination, analgesia, symptom relief, maintain airway, aspirin +/– thrombolysis, achieve calm as much as possible, deal with wife sympathetically, refer to hospital, stay with patient until ambulance arrives.

4 Discretionary. Role of general practitioner in MI, with reference to current literature, importance of ambulance, paramedics, equipment on board, role of thrombolysis, proximity to hospital, stress of emergency medicine in general practice, general practitioners becoming deskilled.

20.5

In evening surgery Mr Alec Baldwin, a 35-year-old travelling salesman, comes to see you. You have been treating him over the past 3 weeks with a persisting chest infection which is slow to resolve with your treatment. Speculate on the reasons for his slow recovery.

CONSTRUCTS

1 Problems with compliance. Awareness of importance of compliance and of factors that affect it – doctor–patient relationship, importance of condition, patient's ideas about medication, etc.

2 Inaccurate diagnosis. Achieving correct diagnosis with aid of history, examination, ? CXR, ? blood tests, ? peak flow, ? spirometry, etc. Awareness of other diagnoses, atypical pneumonia, TB, asthma, malignancy. Inaccurate treatment.

3 Lifestyle/risk factors. Smoking, alcohol, travel, stress, decreased immunity, risk of HIV, e.g. homosexual or heterosexual sex, i.v. drugs, sensitivity of dealing with the latter enquiries.

20.6

Mr John Jefferies, a 31-year-old executive, comes along to ask for a vasectomy. He has been married for 7 years and has two children aged 2 and 4. How do you advise him?

CONSTRUCTS

1 History. Stability of relationship, health of children, genetic factors, current contraception, any problems with this, his relative youth, your own knowledge of family.

2 Options available. Consultant vs. general practitioner, NHS vs. private, importance of timing, e.g. Friday operation, speed of appointment, alternative contraceptive options discussed.

3 Counselling. Need for follow-up, need for testing afterwards, time delay to be sterile, pain, failure rate, informed consent, exploring his concerns, reason for request, cancer risk.

20.7

Your next patient is Mrs Gladys Pound, who is recently bereaved. You looked after her husband, Maurice, at home for his last 3 months with carcinoma of the bronchus. He died peacefully 3 weeks ago. She says, 'I'm sorry to bother you, doctor, but I have a bit of a chesty cough.' How would you wish to carry out this consultation?

CONSTRUCTS

1 Connect. Welcome patient, 'no bother at all!', show warmth, willingness to talk and listen, consultation skills, e.g. use of touch, catharsis, time available, available for follow-up.

2 Assess symptoms. History, examination, importance of cough or just excuse to get to see you, her concerns or worries about cough. Has she had symptoms for long time but didn't want to mention them while husband alive? Explore hidden agenda.

3 Assess bereavement status. What stage of bereavement is she currently at? Awareness of bereavement stages, explanation of stages to patient in terms she understands, assess support in community, family friends, etc., discuss agencies, e.g. CRUSE.

20.8

Your practice nurse asks if you could review your surgery's needle-stick policy. What areas should you cover with her?

CONSTRUCTS

1 Reasons for reviewing policy. Just been on course, being efficient, or has a problem with current policy which brought about this request, danger to patients and staff. Is a review necessary?

2 Avoiding injury. Venesection techniques, resheathing needles, use of gloves, type of sharps boxes, their location and disposal, health and safety at work, labelling high-risk specimens, handling specimens.

3 Avoiding infection. Staff vaccination: who needs it, is it compulsory/ voluntary, are courses completed, are antibody levels checked? Awareness of risk, e.g. HIV, hepatitis B, education for staff/doctors.

4 What to do if injury occurs. Cleaning wound, blood testing, when to do, accident book, defence union, whether passive immunization is necessary, advice from public health microbiologist.

20.9

You receive a letter from a neighbouring general practitioner. She is organizing a co-operative locally to cover out-of-hours care and would like to know if you are interested in joining the co-op once it is set up. How do you respond?

CONSTRUCTS

1 Quality of co-op. What is her reputation like, is she competent? Congratulate her on getting this far. Who is joining, what area is covered, will there be enough doctors, of what quality, enough drivers, administrators, communication facilities, adequate centre to see patients, safety for doctors, traffic?

2 Is there a need? Already deputizing and happy with it, already in a co-op, happy with out-of-hours cover within surgery, present rota, awareness of doctors' stress/health, the future of out-of-hours cover. Is it appropriate, e.g. rural area, too large an area?

3 Commitment needed. How many shifts will you be required to do, can you cope with workload, what will it cost, can you afford it, do you have opportunity to work extra shifts/opt out completely?

4 Decision-making process. Can you make decision as an individual, who else matters, partnership, patients, family, staff? What does partnership agreement say? Possibility for conflict within partnership, how to resolve, practice meeting.

20.10

You agree to give a talk to a small group of medical students on the subject of 'Why you should choose general practice as a career'. What do you wish to include in your talk?

CONSTRUCTS

1 Professional aspects of job. Independent contractor status, no hierarchy among partners, make own decisions for patients, make decisions for partnership, gatekeeper role, 'power', importance of being a partner, partner status easily achieved, fundholding status, role as employer, standing in community, generous income, time management under your control.

2 Patient care. Continuity of care, doctor–patient relationship, family care, patient respect, patient gratitude, successful management plans in your control, getting to grips with difficult patients, patient confidences/trust, generations growing up.

3 Career prospects. Part-time, job-sharing, assistant opportunities, ability to develop own career in any way, e.g. training, course-organizing, medical student, CME, clinical assistantship, other specialities, police surgeon, BASICS, politics, RCGP, fundholding, academic work.

Commentary 20

The surgery deals with some basic general practice problems – difficulty sleeping and tension headaches – but also with some difficult management issues, recent bereavement, needlestick policy, the use of co-operatives and general practice as a career. The constructs include establishing rapport, health beliefs, doctor's agenda, lifestyle, counselling, assessing bereavement status, quality of co-operative and career prospects.